From
MOB TIES To
MIRACLES

A True Story of Betrayal and Redemption

Karen McCormack Haugen

Published by Argyle Fox Publishing | argylefoxpublishing.com

All newspaper articles reprinted with permission from *St. Louis Post-Dispatch*.

Publisher holds no responsibility for content of this work. Content is the sole responsibility of the author.

ISBN 979-8-89124-056-8 (Hardcover)

ARGYLE FOX
PUBLISHING

Dedication

To my wonderful husband, Daniel, whose unwavering support and encouragement inspired me to finally sit down and share this story of betrayal and redemption.

It is my hope that the lessons of my life serve as a light to others, guiding them through their own struggles, and that they may find the same joy and peace in the Father that I have discovered along this long and arduous journey.

TABLE OF CONTENTS

From
MOB TIES To
MIRACLES
A True Story of Betrayal and Redemption

PROLOGUE

IN THE EARLY 1950s, ST. LOUIS, MISSOURI, WAS A VIBRANT symphony of industrious spirit and cultural richness, a city alive with the rhythms of progress. Its history resonated with industries—brewing, flour milling, cattle slaughtering, paper making, machinery manufacturing, tobacco processing, and production of paints, bricks, and iron—each contributing to the city's distinct tapestry. Prominent companies like Ralston Purina, International Shoe, and the Brown Shoe Company proudly called St. Louis home, weaving their own notes into the city's economic melody.

As a musical melting pot, St. Louis pulsated with the energy of blues, ragtime, and jazz, harmonizing with the soaring voices of a renowned choral society and the elegant strains of the St. Louis Symphony. Baseball also played in this rhapsody, with the St. Louis Cardinals maintaining their cherished place in the city's heart since the early 1900s. The completion of the mall park in the 1950s and the commencement of Gateway Arch construction in 1963—financed through city-issued bonds—marked yet another crescendo in St. Louis's evolution, a promise of new beginnings resonating through its streets.

The inner city thrummed with life as a multicultural hub of blue-collar workers drawn from diverse European ancestries—Italian, Irish, German, Czechoslovakian, Yugoslavian, Austrian, Polish, Russian, and Ashkenazi Jews—living alongside the rich contributions of African Americans. Each group, united by dreams of prosperity, blended their unique cultural threads into a shared sense of community. The Soulard Market epitomized this vibrant mosaic, a bustling center where aspirations mingled like the improvisational harmony of a jazz ensemble.

The streets of Soulard mirrored my own search for meaning and purpose. The rhythm of St. Louis life, much like its jazz, carried both harmony and dissonance, hinting at challenges ahead. Little did I know that the city's industrious spirit, diverse melodies, and interwoven cultures would reflect the trials and triumphs shaping my path.

St. Louis was more than a backdrop—it was a crucible where my story began. The hum of factories, soulful strains of blues, and whispers of shared dreams framed my earliest memories. Here, in the heart of America, the seeds of my journey were planted—a journey defined by ambition, loss, faith, and the pursuit of something greater.

ACT I

THE EARLY YEARS

CHAPTER I

A ST. LOUIS CHILDHOOD IN THE SHADOW OF THE MOB

"That ye may be the children of your Father which is in heaven: for he maketh his sun to rise on the evil and on the good, and sendeth rain on the just and on the unjust."—Matthew 5:45

THE TV ANNOUNCER BROKE THE PEACE AND TRANQUILITY of the evening with two words:

"Jack McCormack . . ."

My head whipped toward the black-and-white TV, my heart pounding. I could hardly believe it—his day of reckoning had arrived. The words rang out loud and clear, freezing me in place. My hands turned cold as I stared, transfixed. Why were they talking about him? What was happening?

I watched strangers on the screen lift a stretcher shrouded with a white sheet, sliding it into the coroner's vehicle. Beneath that sheet lay my father, Jack McCormack, silent and still, his presence extinguished from our lives in an instant.

". . . ex-convict," the announcer continued, "the reputed 'brains' of the Anheuser Busch Credit Union robbery . . ."

I felt the words before the announcer spoke them.

". . . has just been fatally shot."

The words were a death blow, killing any innocence my childhood retained.

Aunt Frances snatched the telephone from the vanity and frantically spun the rotary to phone my grandmother. It all felt like a bad movie or a bad dream, but there was no waking up, no walking out after the show. This was my reality.

My father's mob ties had drawn us into the dark glamour of the St. Louis underworld, painting illusions of prestige and a life wrapped in gilded promises. Fame, as it turned out, was merely a veil contrived by forces opposed to light—a deceptive illusion conjured by the agents of darkness.

The dreams of a grand life were nothing more than hollow echoes, resonating in empty chambers of power and control. In the end, my father gave everything—including his life—for that treacherous mirage.

Fortunately, this wasn't the whole story. No, this story is still being written to this day, with miracles sprinkled along every page. And despite the odds, it has a happy ending. But let's not get ahead of ourselves. Let's start at the top—or the top as defined by my memory.

• • •

My grandparents resided on Hickory Street, just two miles to the Mississippi River. Their home was a two-story brick structure that housed two flats, each boasting three spacious rooms. The kitchen, dominated by a large rustic wooden table, shared space with a modest bathroom. The middle room served as a practical hub, featuring a small black-and-white television, my grandfather's cherished rocking chair—perpetually occupied during episodes of *Gunsmoke*, *Roy Rogers*, and *The Rifleman*—and a scattering of bedroom furniture. My grandparents' bedroom, positioned at the front, offered a quiet retreat from the bustling world outside, where their complexities of life unfolded in everyday moments.

Grandpa Roy was a self-taught artist with an extraordinary passion for creation, transforming everyday materials into art that spoke of skill and imagination. His talents ranged from sculpting delicate figurines to experimenting with a spectrum of painting mediums, including charcoal and oil paints. Each stroke and carve seemed to channel a boundless creativity, driven by a deep love for expressing beauty and emotion through his work.

One might say he had a particular artistic "focus," as his fascination with the female form found its way into many of his works, much to the bemusement of those who knew him. Grandpa's pieces, often shaped by this admiration for the so-called gentler sex, raised an eyebrow or two. Despite Grandpa's female form-focused artistic inclinations, his bond with my grandmother was unmistakable. Their affection for each other was as open and passionate as Grandpa's art, though Nana—ever modest in public—sometimes blushed at Grandpa's more ardent displays of appreciation.

At the rear of their apartment, a creaking wooden staircase led to a small patio. I often sat in the yard below, enveloped in the hush of early evening, surrounded by mingling fragrances of damp earth and blooming roses. A stately Yellowwood tree stood as my steadfast companion, its branches laden with fragrant white blossoms. Beneath that leafy canopy, I found solace—a fragile shelter from the fractured world around me.

Life moved slowly in the humid summer months, the scent of hops from Anheuser-Busch blending with the smoky haze of industrial pollution. My grandparents' neighborhood was shaped by the region's abundant clay deposits. Artisans molded the clay into bricks, giving rise to the sturdy homes and buildings that defined the neighborhood's character and charm, creating a life uniquely tied to the land itself.

St. Louis in the '50s sprawled like a rust-colored tapestry—worn brick houses with straight edges softened by uneven cobblestones below. Towering trees stretched boldly against a vibrant, ever-changing blue sky, a balance of straight and crooked, much like the people who lived there. Each resident, with their flaws and strengths, was woven into the city's enduring, rough-hewn fabric.

The streets were alive with the tantalizing aromas of international cuisines—pasta, potatoes, garlic, and onions, all seasoned to perfection by families from diverse backgrounds. Street vendors added to the aroma and noise.

Saturday mornings held a sleepy quiet, undisturbed until the sight and sounds of the arabbers —horse-drawn cart vendors who had rambled down the urban cobblestone streets for generations. Their brightly painted carts rattled as they called out their wares in a rich, singsong timbre: "Watermelon! Watermelon!" Their voices echoed through the stillness, stirring a flurry of activity as people hurried to exchange wrinkled dollar bills and carefully counted change for fresh fruits and vegetables.

Despite our poverty, I never imagined that life should be—or could be—any different. At just four years old, as a little girl, my perspective was limited to the immediate circumstances enveloping me. My world was small, parochial, and free from contemplations on the meaning of life or the possibility of a better world elsewhere.

One of life's simple treasures came in the form of hot tamales. We'd catch their scent before the vendor's cart came into view, the air filling with the delicious aroma as he called out, "Hot tamales, hot tamales!" Behind his three-wheeled cart, he'd draw a crowd, our mouths watering as we lined up for another round. At three for ten cents, it was an indulgence we could hardly pass up.

Just as the tamale vendor's call would fade down the block, another familiar figure would roll in, pedaling his clanking, rattling cart. With a symphony of bells and whirring belts, the knife sharpener brought his own flair to the street, offering to sharpen knives, saws, scissors, and tools. I never quite understood why he needed to make such a racket, but his presence, loud as it was, became part of the neighborhood's character—a lively rhythm of our everyday world.

On trash days, the streets were cluttered with battered galvanized steel trash cans. The lids, so dented they never fit properly, constantly fell off, adding to the cacophony of never-ending sound. Neighbors leaned out of their double-hung windows and called to friends and family: "Yoohoo, Annie, can you come out?" Knocking on doors seemed too formal, and many families didn't have a telephone.

Our new clothes, when we were fortunate enough to have any, were always itchy. My first pair of blue jeans were so stiff and rigid they made me feel like the Tin Man trying to do the cha-cha with rusty joints. They were so uncomfortable I avoided them until my teens.

In those years, DDT was touted as a miracle for preventing malaria, typhus, and other insect-borne diseases. Trucks drove through the streets, spraying the stuff without discrimination, leaving behind a thick, pesticide-laden fog. Kids chased the trucks on their bikes, weaving through the mist as if in some strange, chemical cloud parade. On the surface, it seemed like a fairytale, but that fog led many to nagging challenges and even devastation.

A few miles from my grandparents' home was the St. Louis Zoo, where Phil the gorilla lived—renowned for his playful tricks and weighing in at a staggering 776 pounds, the largest gorilla in captivity. Phil had a knack for swiping the zookeeper's beer and smoking discarded cigarettes, looking like an oversized child caught between mischief and curiosity. Everyone adored him, and he seemed to thrive on the attention, always eager for the crowd's interaction. The irony wasn't lost on me: here I was, captivated in my own way, feeling an unexpected kinship with this giant spirit. Trapped in my own world, unable to fully break free, I saw a reflection of my own restlessness in Phil—his longing for something more, the need to reach beyond the bars, even if only for a fleeting moment.

I don't recall anyone reaching the end of their days, but St. Louis took care of the poor. Occasionally, we heard whispers about someone forced to go to the dreaded City Hospital, the place reserved for those without insurance or financial means. The mere mention of it sent shivers down our spines, as if Death loomed ominously over every unfortunate soul who entered.

We often window-shopped at Famous Bar. If we had enough money to make a purchase, we watched in awe as the sales slip and cash traveled up large pneumatic tubes to the second floor to the cashier, our change soon returning the same way. It was a marvel of technology, the tubes whooshing our money away and returning change in a matter of moments.

The cosmetics counter always drew a crowd, where the most popular shade, "Cherries in the Snow," seemed to be worn by every blonde and brunette Marilyn Monroe and Jane Russell type.

We often visited my mother's friend, Jonette Rubinstein, who lived nearby. She was beautiful, with the mysterious allure of Sophia Loren. Despite her financial struggles and an abusive husband, Jonette exuded class and resilience. Her home was filled with music from an RCA tabletop radio that played hits by Ella Fitzgerald, Frank Sinatra, Peggy Lee, and Doris Day. Jonette's loyalty to her family was unwavering, though her husband, Stephanco, made her cry a lot.

Anne Perica was nearly part of the family, a constant companion and my mother's very best friend. She had an uncanny ability to make us laugh so hard we couldn't stop, tears running down our faces, as we begged her to stop the jokes and our consequent bellyaching. Now, I suppose laughter kept us sane and able to cope, because it seemed the only pastime we truly pursued.

• • •

Organized crime was rampant in the U.S. during the 1940s and 1950s. The St. Louis Mafia dates back to the mid-1890s with the emergence of Italian Mafia gangs. The St. Louis crime family, also known as the Giordano crime family, was involved in a range of illegal activities, including racketeering, bribery, murder, loansharking, extortion, drug trafficking, bookmaking, and illegal gambling. The Giordanos allied with other powerful crime syndicates—the Kansas City crime family, the Chicago Outfit, the Detroit Partnership, and the Cleveland crime family. Notable figures included Frank "Buster" Wortman, a bootlegger and gang leader with extensive political connections.

Additionally, the Hogan Gang, primarily composed of Irish Americans, operated out of Hogan's Saloon. Members included Humbert Costello, Charles Mercurio, Leo Casey, and Patrick Scanlon.

One year before my birth, in September 1953, six-year-old Bobby Greenlease was kidnapped from Notre Dame de Sion, a Catholic school in Kansas City, and subsequently murdered. His father, Robert Cosgrove Greenlease Sr., was a multimillionaire auto dealer, and the demanded ransom was the largest in American history at the time. We all knew about the murder because the mob was ingrained in our culture and heritage. The mob's continual presence forced us to live in a constant flight-or-fight scenario, and the story brought fear home to us, making us realize how close we were to real, life-altering, life-ending violence. Bobby Greenlease's murder served as a stark reminder of the dangers lurking in our own neighborhood, highlighting the pervasive and insidious influence of organized crime.

My connection to the mob began here, amidst the backdrop of a city straining to build a better future under the pervasive influence of organized crime. Some of my facts may not be historically perfect, as I was very young when these things happened, but with these stories, I faithfully relay what I heard and saw.

• • •

My mother met my father, Jack, in 1951, when she was just seventeen. He stood tall, towering over her petite five-foot-two frame, his commanding presence capped off with piercing steel-blue eyes. With an unwavering determination to pursue his desires, Jack would stop at nothing to achieve his goals, a force that drew my mother in from the moment they met.

They met at Club Imperial Dance Hall, a glamorous venue that featured acts like Ike & Tina Turner, Chuck Berry, and Bob Kuban and the In-Men. The ballroom hosted swing bands such as the Stan Kenton Orchestra and Louis Prima.

By the mid-1950s, rhythm and blues was taking over the city as the world discovered the exciting bands emerging from across the river. The St. Louis music scene attracted black and white audiences, with beloved St. Louis musician and radio personality DJ Gabriel recalling, "Ike Turner just took over this area. He created a ripple effect with his energy and ambition, and premier blues musicians followed him from Mississippi."

In the 1950s, a type of swing dance known as the "Imperial Style" originated at Club Imperial, where the Tommy Clements Dance Studio was located. It was easy to get swept up in the glamour of this emerging era of new music and trends, with iconic musicians originating here. Any young couple would have succumbed to the charm, energy, and romance of it all. So, it's no wonder it was love at first sight for Wilma and Jack.

From the moment they met, an undeniable spark ignited between these two passionate, lonely Irish souls. When Jack invited Wilma to Louisiana for Mardi Gras, she fibbed to her mother, claiming she was spending time with a friend. The trip became a dreamlike escape, her first real adventure away from home. Their whirlwind courtship was brief but intense, lasting only two weeks before Jack proposed.

Their chemistry was electric—an instant fire, an unmistakable passion. From the moment their eyes met, it was clear that this kind of love was rare. As I look back and gather the fragments of my memories, I sometimes wonder if a flame can burn so intensely that it feels almost divine—a passion so fierce, so consuming, that it seems almost too much for human hearts to endure.

Jack's fierce intensity wasn't limited to romance; it also extended to his life on the streets. Like a character from a classic mob tale, he was sharp, astute, and adept at outwitting adversaries. Raised by a struggling single mother, his early years were marked by abandonment and hardship. By fifteen, after rejection from his mother and stepfather, he found himself in a life of crime, searching for belonging and power. Though hardened and desensitized, Jack never lost sight of the moral implications of his choices—a tension that defined him to the end.

My mother, Wilma, was a natural beauty who carried an alluring naïveté and sharp intellect. She was gifted with the wisdom of the righteous, yet unafraid to fly as close to the sun as possible. Young and inexperienced, she was reserved, self-conscious, oblivious to her own delicate charm and lovability.

Upon graduating from high school, she yearned to gain independence from the constant rampage at home. My mother feared her parents' raging shouting matches as my grandmother slammed her hands on the kitchen table and sent dishes flying, her fury as dangerous as an exploding freight train.

In the midst of the chaos, she fostered her infinite talent for writing music and playing musical instruments. By the age of seven, weekends included trips to a local radio station, where she played piano and Hawaiian guitar for live broadcasts.

With such publicity, Wilma eagerly awaited the moment she would become all she was meant to be. Perhaps, she thought, fame and stardom would be hers as an accomplished musician, actress, model, or—could it be true?—a treasured wife and mother!

Jack, nine years her senior, promised the fulfillment of all her dreams. In the heady rush of young love, he couldn't wait to make Wilma his own. Taking him at his word and not knowing anything about the good-looking, mysterious big spender, she excitedly agreed to his marriage proposal.

They eloped to Arkansas, sealing their love officially.

When she returned home to introduce her new husband to her parents, Hester and Roy were furious. Roy even threatened Jack with a shotgun. However, Jack's calming words and undeniable charm convinced them to lower their weapons. Over time, they reluctantly accepted the young man who had run off and married their daughter, though they always kept a watchful eye on him.

Jack's six-foot-two physique and effervescent charm made him a commanding presence at any gathering. His energy and charisma elicited a strong emotional response from everyone around him. Self-confident, gregarious, and brimming with boundless energy and impetuous humor, Jack captivated with his grand schemes and knack for navigating adventure and the impossible.

Always impeccably dressed, Jack effortlessly won admiration and appreciation. He harbored a deep desire to be a devoted family man, fiercely protective of his wife and children. Despite this, my mother, Wilma, often said, "Jack wanted so much to love but never knew how and could only love as much as he was able."

Highly analytical and never one to lose an argument, Jack had a broad perspective that fueled both his convictions and his eloquent gaming strategies. He approached discussions like a chess match, always thinking several moves ahead and thriving on the mental "dance" that engaged his cunning wit. With quick humor and a persuasive charm, he won over even the brightest minds, often leaving them marveling at the rhetorical path he had led them down. Debate was his game, and he played to win, yet those around him couldn't help but love him for it.

Jack's passions weren't limited to words; he had a deep love for the saxophone, perhaps drawn to its ability to capture the full spectrum of emotions he kept so carefully hidden. The saxophone could wail with the raw intensity of the blues or flow smoothly through a jazz ballad, mirroring Jack's own complex inner life. In its haunting notes, he found a rare peace, as though the instrument spoke his own unspoken thoughts. It was his musical escape, a way to express the depths of his spirit beyond the clever words he wielded so expertly.

He kept his troubled past hidden, concealing four years behind bars for narcotics sales and gambling, along with a daring escape from a juvenile detention facility at fifteen. None of that would have mattered to my mother anyway.

Unbeknownst to him, she sought a savior—a way out of the chaos and misery of her upbringing. Her heart yearned for the serenity of her childhood with Aunt Lindy in Farmington, a dream she clung to amidst the turmoil of Hickory Street. She craved Jack's attention and flattery, longing to spend her days with this enigmatic, emotionally captivating man. Little did she know the turbulence awaiting her would surpass any she'd known.

Their union lacked the bliss of a honeymoon and was instead marked by a swift return to St. Louis. My mother worked tirelessly as a model at the Brown Shoe Company, coming home exhausted from standing all day, while Jack disappeared into the night as a cab driver. Loneliness crept in, eroding the romance she had hoped for. His absences soon led to a run-in with the law that resulted in jail time for stolen cars and parts. Despite the abundance of evidence, Jack vehemently denied any wrongdoing.

Promises of a fresh start surged with his release from custody, invigorated by the arrival of me, their first child. Jack appeared transformed—attentive and devoted.

My parents were once again blissfully entwined, dreaming of a future filled with possibility. Their days sparkled with playful energy, laughter, and joy found in simple moments that transformed the mundane into the extraordinary.

• • •

With the arrival of their second child, my mother faced physical exhaustion and financial strain. She continued working while worrying about my grandma's ability to care for my sister, Mary, and me, and Jack's increasingly lengthy absences. Determined, she purchased a tavern and worked long hours to support us. Jack made sporadic visits, promising change, and his joyful appearances brought laughter and warmth into our home. Striving for independence from my grandparents, my mother moved us to a flat on Chippewa Street, resolute to start anew—with Jack or without.

Occasionally, Jack called out of loneliness, and my mother never said no. Lacking understanding of the dynamics of a healthy relationship, my mother was committed to life with Jack, regardless of its dysfunction. Divorce was never a consideration she had the luxury of considering. She was too absorbed in living and surviving. Despite the challenges, Jack truly loved us, his love often expressed through grand gestures, like the day he drove up in a breathtaking fire-engine red convertible Cadillac. Excited, we hopped in and raced away to show it off, offering rides to Nana and Grandpa Roy.

When Jack was with us, it felt as if he belonged entirely, wholly to us.

There were moments when he cast aside his grown-up seriousness, dropped to the floor, and joined us in our playful antics. Maybe he wanted to relive his childhood vicariously, so he—a grown man I soon learned was a dangerous man—determinedly mastered hopscotch in a bid to win our hearts. His impulsive streak frequently led us on whimsical city adventures, from impromptu picnics in Forest Park to spontaneous games that felt straight out of a slapstick comedy. Those times brought a blend of laughter and yearning, a reminder of the man who, despite his frequent absence, was my father.

The first Christmas Eve I remember was filled with wonder and pure delight. Mommy and Daddy moved up and down the hollow-sounding wooden staircase, their laughter and chatter echoing warmly through the apartment. Pretending to be asleep, I listened with eager anticipation, my heart racing as I heard them stumbling and dropping boxes in excitement. Each sound—a thud, a shuffle—was a joyful reminder of the magic unfolding. It was as if their own delight in preparing for the big day outshone our excitement for the gifts themselves. This night, full of promise and enchantment, would forever remain woven into the fabric of my childhood memories.

On Christmas morning, the air was thick with anticipation. The crisp winter chill seeped through the cracks of our cozy upstairs apartment, where the scent of fresh pine from the tree filled the room, mingling with the pure, unembellished freshness of the morning. There was no gingerbread to sweeten the air, just the simplicity of our modest surroundings—a reminder that joy didn't come from extravagance, but from the warmth of being together.

Beautifully wrapped packages lay scattered, each one a promise waiting to be unwrapped. As I suspiciously studied my gifts, I wondered if my most frequent petition would be granted.

After an eternity of waiting, I tore open the largest package and beheld the most exquisite porcelain bride doll ever imagined. She had a delicate porcelain face with intricate features, a flowing white lace dress, and a shimmering veil. I held her close and took in her faint, sweet fragrance, then named her Sophia, after Italian actress Sophia Loren.

The immense surprise and joy overwhelmed me, creating a unique, serene moment in which both my parents were present—when Jack wasn't "doing his thing" and Mom wasn't working.

Sometimes, my parents worked together at home. Our apartment was small, but the tall ceilings gave the feeling of spaciousness.

There was always endless laundry and ironing. My mother ironed clothes from a basket after first sprinkling water on each cotton piece to smooth the wrinkles. The iron's long cord extended to the ceiling, where it was plugged into the light bulb socket, the light swaying gently as my mother ironed.

Our wringer washing machine had an agitator that moved back and forth, forcing water through the clothes to remove dirt. After washing, we fed each wet piece of clothing through the wringer to squeeze out the extra water before hanging the clothing on the line to dry.

Other washings were more delicate.

I have vivid memories of my parents washing paper currency, following in the footsteps of a generation of launderers. During the Prohibition Era of the 1920s and 1930s, criminals in the illegal alcohol trade needed ways to launder cash. Organized crime groups, like those led by Al Capone, used legitimate businesses such as laundromats to "clean" their profits, coining the term "money laundering." Fitting, as many of the banknotes they handled were marked.

My parents washed paper money and hung the notes to dry on a clothesline stretched across the kitchen, using wooden clothespins. I found it amusing and felt a strange sense of empowerment, as if we had reached a new level in life. Despite the seemingly harmless nature of my parents washing and drying U.S. currency in the kitchen, I couldn't shake the feeling that something was amiss.

Anytime Nana or my mother mentioned our "need for an infusion of cash," Jack would promptly vanish, as if off to close a deal on Wall Street—secretive, fast, and always returning with a wad of wet, moldy bills, leaving us all scratching our heads. It was like something out of *Nice Work If You Can Get It*—if you can get it, that is. And if you can, won't you tell me how?

Family and friends couldn't help but speculate, whispering that Jack might have known the whereabouts of the missing money from the Greenlease kidnapping—a staggering $300,000 (roughly $3.4 million today)—money that was never recovered. Some even spun tales of the cash being buried beneath the murky Meramec River, while others imagined it hidden away in an abandoned airplane hangar, awaiting its eventual discovery. I've often wondered if Jack's mysterious disappearances were somehow tied to that infamous crime during his time as a cab driver, though no one could ever say for sure.

Why didn't he take all of it? It surely wasn't making interest. Maybe he fancied himself a modern-day Robin Hood or had grand plans he never got to carry out. We'll never know. The possibilities are endless, adding a touch of intrigue to Jack's colorful character.

• • •

At the end of the political Reconstruction, the rise of the Ku Klux Klan in the South compelled many Southern Blacks to migrate north to cities such as St. Louis. Perhaps most famous among these migrants were the Exodusters, so named for their exodus to what they saw as their American promised land. Race relations in St. Louis were more complex than in many places, due to its location in a border state. As more Black families arrived, schools and neighborhoods increasingly moved toward segregation.

After World War II, the Black population in St. Louis surged, making up ninety-five percent of some neighborhoods. A growing effort to desegregate communities and promote African American culture and equal opportunity coincided with escalating tensions between inner city Blacks and Whites. For instance, the Veiled Prophet organization did not allow Black members. It was founded in 1878 as an all-male secret society for select civic and governmental leaders. Elitism and discrimination lead to demonstrations pressuring banks and utility companies to hire Blacks. Local skirmishes and clashes between Whites and Blacks became more frequent.

• • •

In the summer of 1958, my mother was pregnant with her third child, and my father's visits were brief and infrequent. During this time, Nana regularly took me to the library. Walking down Gravois Avenue, immersed in the damp smells of the city and the sounds of bustling traffic, was a beautiful and special time with her. An avid reader, she found solace in books, as they transported her to distant lands and fueled her curious mind. Though not college-educated, she was highly intelligent and largely self-taught, devoting countless hours to reading and constantly expanding her understanding of the world.

I cherished the moments she held my hand, our arms swinging like schoolgirl friends. We shared a love for the smell of books, the sound of footsteps on rich wooden floors, and the librarian's respectful whisper, bonding over the vast world found between the covers of those books. We also found joy beyond the library in the most unusual places. Drawn by the boisterous excitement of a four-alarm fire, we once stood in awe as a two-story brownstone was engulfed in flames, joining the neighborhood to witness the drama. Those were the simple, thrilling entertainments of the time.

My grandparents were deeply involved in the Masons and the Masonic Order of the Eastern Star, organizations known for their exclusivity and secrecy, particularly toward nonmembers and African Americans. This air of loyalty and mystery surrounding membership intrigued me and left me uncomfortable. My grandmother encouraged me to join the Masonic youth organization Job's Daughters International, but membership never appealed to me.

Nana prepared for their grand ball events, the kind of lavish parties where society's elite gathered to celebrate. Always meticulously prepared, my grandmother was an elected member of the Eastern Star, a title she wore with pride and reverence. Dressing in exquisite gowns and adorning herself with pearls, she transformed into a figure of sophistication. Before dashing off, she sat gracefully in the living room's upholstered tub chair, her arms draped over the sides, a cigarette in one hand and a rhinestone bracelet glittering on the other. Her rich chestnut brown hair was impeccably styled, permed, and colored—a living portrait of Elizabeth Taylor, her big, brown, almond shaped-eyes and artfully sculpted eyebrows lending a captivating, elegant expression.

Living in a neighborhood where crime was as routine as Sunday pot roast, Nana carried a small pistol tucked in her satin clutch. "Karen," she called to me, our bond unbreakable since I was the oldest. I could hardly contain my joy when she sought my attention. "Do you want to see something?" she asked. I was drawn to her mysterious allure.

With a flourish, Nana opened her clutch to reveal a pocket derringer nestled beside a tube of striking ruby red lipstick. She was ready to kill with charm or the pull of a trigger.

At our home on Chippewa Street, the remnants of Jack's chaotic life lingered, a constant presence that haunted us. A blinking blue-and-white light outside our second-floor, three-room apartment—just beyond the play area—served as an ever-present reminder of the tumult we were living through. One night, that fragile peace was shattered by a sharp, jarring noise from outside. Peering through the window, I saw a strange man in dark clothing, desperately trying to pry open a window that overlooked the fire escape. It was clear to us that he was likely after my father, perhaps due to his ties to the mob, or worse, he might have been targeting my mother or one of us. Our frantic commotion scared him off, but it left us with an unsettling realization—life in our home was fraught with dangers we couldn't escape.

In urban St. Louis, the constant fear of crime and racial tensions loomed. One evening in the summer heat when tensions were high, a band of African American rabble-rousers confronted my mother, looking for a fight. My mother, exhilarated by the potential clash and eager to prove her superior gamesmanship, engaged them. Fortunately, after a few cocky words, the altercation ended, and we went about our evening.

The following Friday evening, the air was thick with tension as a mob gathered outside our apartment. Their presence stretched several blocks, as far as I could see, like an ominous wave of unrest rolling through the night. The leader's voice rang out, demanding that my mother come to them. The mob's anger was palpable, and in the thick of it, we feared the worst, assuming they had something far darker in mind—perhaps a lynching.

As the chants escalated, my Aunt Mary held me tight, and we fled to a small grocer behind the building. She used the old stand-up phone, frantically summoning the police to come as soon as possible. A riot was beginning to develop, she explained, and lives were at risk. We were in dire distress.

Moments later, a siren sounded. Police were always nearby and ready—there was always someone being engaged by law enforcement. I watched through my four-year-old eyes as the police car arrived and the crowd vanished. It was a portent and bold statement of our vulnerability, and we could no longer live here—not safely.

The summer seemed to never end, and Jack wouldn't leave us alone.

One afternoon my mother questioned him, and his evasive answers led to a shouting match. It escalated quickly. Lamps were thrown and screams echoed through the flat. Amid the chaos, I—in all my diminutive but bold stature—screamed for them to stop, even threatening to intervene. They ignored my threats. Jack slammed my mother to the floor, her eye already swollen black and blue as she unsuccessfully shielded herself against his blows.

Eventually, Jack stormed out in a rage. My mother swore this would be the last time. Shaky yet composed, she promised this would be the end of Jack McCormack, that he would never hurt us again. I desperately wanted to believe her. I felt relief, but it was clear—we needed a change.

Nearly six months later, Jack reappeared behind the wheel of a gleaming yellow Cadillac Coupe de Ville. Despite their struggles and the passage of time, it was clear that the flame between them had never extinguished. When my mother saw Jack, her resolve melted away, and he, too, couldn't wait to reunite.

Along with the new car, Jack arrived with briefcases brimming with money and keys to a new house in the suburbs. His return was nothing short of divine elation. Seeing him again filled our hearts with a warmth that was both exhilarating and comforting. His sometimes-silly antics and unpredictable nature, while often painful, were familiar, and our hearts melted at the sight of him. He yearned for our love, eager to create a safe haven for us. How could we resist such an offer? With excitement bubbling over, we packed and moved to our new home on Cranberry Lane. Our joy was overwhelming, made complete with a backyard that came with not one but two boxer dogs, Fritz and Ricky, companions to guard us and make every day an adventure.

Our new house provided a brief but welcome escape from the chaos of city life. My mother beamed with creativity, dressing me in exquisite handmade clothes that made me the envy of my entire kindergarten class. She crafted outfits with heavily starched, white French cuffs, matching accessories, and elegant buttons, ensuring I always stood out. But even in this peaceful bubble, there were moments that jolted me back to the spectacle of our life.

Jack once came home with a Mr. Softee ice cream truck and invited every neighborhood child over for free ice cream. While the kids were thrilled with his generosity, a wave of embarrassment washed over me. The loud, flashy display felt more like a spectacle than a genuine act of kindness. Jack always needed to show his generosity in the most ostentatious ways, and though his heart was in the right place, it often left me feeling awkward and out of place.

These feelings surfaced during family outings as well. Each year, my father took us to St. Louis's high-end department stores, Stix Baer & Fuller and Famous-Barr, to see the holiday lights and decorations. The sights, fragrances, and melodies of Christmas filled the air as we wandered through the stores, everything magical and enchanting. An entire floor dedicated to Santa and Toyland felt glorious and, for a child with little means, almost divine. But my dreams often found me lost in that setting, feeling forlorn. Those magical moments left me with an unrelenting sense of longing and unfinished hopes. Beneath the surface, there was always a sadness knowing those lovely things were never meant for me.

At our new home, we spent endless afternoons playing hopscotch, double Dutch jump rope, and freeze tag. I was captivated by glass marbles, their vibrant colors and intricate patterns sparking my imagination. The thrill of opening a box of Breeze powdered detergent to find a free dish towel and the anticipation of saving S&H Green Stamps added excitement to everyday life. We carefully collected each stamp, with gummed back, and pasted it into a book. When the book was full, we exchanged it for housewares or other treasures at the Green Stamps store. The search for those final elusive stamps was a thrilling quest, and redeeming them felt like a grand achievement. Happiness was truly found in these small, insignificant pleasures.

Despite Jack's joyous return, grand gestures, and the festive atmosphere he manufactured, a lingering sadness often tainted the experiences he contrived. Beneath the seemingly perfect suburban facade was an undercurrent of turmoil that made me question why, amidst such delight, a sense of unfulfilled yearning tugged at my heart.

Meanwhile, Jack's ambitions grew too large for silence. He loved to boast about his schemes and clever prowess, one which involved a very large sum of money. It seemed so grand, so daring. Instinctively, I knew him well, and it was going to be epic. We would either punctuate our former life with a wonderful new one or it would end in futility, as it often did. "If something happens to me," he confided to my mother, "you need to know where the money is stashed." Much to his disappointment, my mother vehemently rejected his offer.

Soon afterward, things got chaotic at home. My parents often began their evenings with shouting matches, both determined to win the argument. These arguments frequently escalated into physical fights, ending with Jack storming out and leaving my mother crying for hours. I did my best to console and comfort her. The last time Jack left us, we were destitute—no transportation and no money for groceries. I felt helpless and wanted to make it all better at the ripe age of six. If only he had left on a peaceful note, just once. But no, his departures always came with a sharp thud, deepening our despair, a heavy silence that seemed to foreshadow his final, tragic departure—a leave-taking not to be followed by a return.

One Saturday, my mother was inconsolable. She cried uncontrollably for hours before retreating to her bedroom, where she collapsed from exhaustion, leaving the remaining laundry unsorted and a box of powdered detergent on the floor. My two-year-old sister, just learning to walk and explore, found the box, tipped it over, and began playing in it as if it were a sandbox.

Alarmed, I ran to tell my mother, only to find her unconscious and unresponsive. An empty bottle of pills lay on her bedside table. "Mommy!" I screamed, shaking her with all my might. She didn't move, so I raced next door to our neighbor, Martha Kehans. Martha followed me and tried to get my mother to drink a glass of water, while

I held her head up. Miraculously, my mother began spitting up, and Martha called 911.

Soon, the ambulance arrived, its siren fading as strangers entered our home and carried my mother's body out on a gurney. That image settled deeply into my memory, remaining clear even after many years. It comes to mind with surprising ease, as if no time has passed, and it lingers softly, a quiet presence in my thoughts as I write this. The details have remained with me, a memory that continues to quietly shape my reflections, even after all this time.

Helpless, I wondered if my mother would ever come home. Would she survive and return home? My eyes fixated on her motionless form, filled with disbelief. What would happen to my two sisters and me? How could I take care of us, when I was just a girl myself? Why would she betray us? Jack's departures were expected, but this—this felt like a deeper betrayal. Didn't she love us? Didn't we mean anything to her? What was I going to do?

But there was no time for pain or sorrow. I had to take control and feign strength. I coped by pretending it was all a dream. I wanted to cry at the weight of the world that fell on my shoulders. I knew things would never be the same. Even as a child, I sensed we would be leaving Cranberry Lane. My parents' fire finally died, snuffed out, leaving only silence and ashes where there once was heat and fury, taking the glimmer of hope Cranberry Lane brought with it.

CHAPTER 2

BIKES, BEATS, AND NAKED LADY HUBCAPS: A SUMMER OF SERENITY

In the serenity of summer, we find a place where warmth and safety prevail, even amidst storms. It's a haven where love makes the skies perpetually bright, shielding hearts from worry. This special place isn't tied to a place but is found wherever friends and family share their dreams, hopes, and love. It's a state of bliss, where even in the midst of challenges, the embrace of a loved one makes everything feel just right.

ONCE THE DUST SETTLED AND MY MOTHER BEGAN TO recover, she was physically and mentally exhausted from dealing with Jack. She was moving forward without him and was convinced Bevo Mill, a neighborhood in south St. Louis, was the place for us. With anticipation and resolve, we drove up and down the streets until she spotted a small "For Rent" sign in the window of a two-story brick flat.

The neighborhood featured tree-lined streets, meticulously manicured two-story brownstones, and charming, postage-stamp-sized green areas. The air of tranquility was broken only by the sounds of children playing and families strolling along the perfectly paved sidewalks. Our new home was within walking distance of our new school and a little church where I learned about Jesus at vacation Bible school. There, in our apartment at the corner of Alaska and Itaska, we felt an indescribable sense of relief and renewal.

I ran through the newly painted three-room flat, my feet and voice echoing off the walls and the twelve-foot ceilings. Double hung windows poured light into the apartment and gave a picture-perfect view of our lovely neighborhood. There was no need to live in secrecy by covering the windows. They were left wide open and uncovered. My two sisters, Mary and Linda, and I shared a bedroom with my mother, energized with our newfound freedom.

• • •

The thoughts of my father faded in the months that followed. We broke free of his spell and were truly free. While the winds of destiny demanded I see him one more time under strange circumstances, that was in the unknown future. In the meantime, a new figure captured our imaginations and hearts.

Watching him on our new television, I felt an instant, familial-like connection to John F. Kennedy. A captivating, appealing Irish charmer, he was sometimes called Jack, like my father. I was only six years old, unable to grasp the breadth and scope of his speeches, but his promises and lofty dreams fed something in my soul. The timing of his arrival on the political stage felt personal, each word spoken in his south Boston accent confirming a new era was unfolding.

Amidst the whirlwind of social change and cultural transformation brought on by the 1960s, Elvis Presley recorded "It's Now or Never" and "Are You Lonesome Tonight." The romance of these two songs swept me off my feet. My mother took me to see Jimmy Bachus in *Snow White and the Seven Dwarfs* at the Granada Movie Theater. I was so smitten that I dreamed Jimmy Bachus kissed me on the knee. Yes, my knee. Even in my dreams, I was aiming low!

St. Louis in the 1960s was a hub of glamour and musical innovation. Chubby Checker popularized the Twist dance style with "Let's Twist" and suddenly, everyone was twisting with wild abandon—young and old engaged in a dance fever dream! *American Bandstand* was the hottest thing on TV, and we all picked up the jitterbug from it.

My mother, grandmother, and their friends recounted their glamorous outings, making me ache to join them on their nights out. St. Louis offered everything from lively dance clubs and live music venues to elegant lounges. Known for its jazz heritage, the city was alive with locals and visitors seeking and savoring exquisite food and expertly crafted cocktails. Gaslight Square, the crown jewel of St. Louis nightlife, sparkled with sophistication, hosting legends like Miles Davis and attracting crowds who mingled alongside celebrities. The Breckenridge Ballroom, Crystal Palace, and Stardust Club at the Chase Park Plaza further enriched the city's dynamic scene.

Though the district began to decline in the late 1960s due to business feuds and rising crime, the vibrant energy of its heyday drew the attention and participation of the mob.

Carondelet Park was our winter wonderland, where we laughed and ice skated on the frozen pond among snow-covered trees. The Hill, St. Louis's Little Italy, enchanted us with authentic Italian restaurants, bakeries, and markets, stuffing the air with the aroma of fresh bread and simmering tomato sauce. Tower Grove Park's Victorian pavilions and lush gardens offered a serene retreat for picnics, strolls, and outdoor concerts. The St. Louis Hop brought lively evenings of jitterbugging and swing dancing.

My dear Aunt Mary stood out as a living embodiment of the time's elegance and charm. She inherited the signature beauty of the Dickey family, with my grandmother's "Dickey" eyes—big, brown, and shaped like almonds—making her a vision of grace. At just sixteen, she carried her five-foot hourglass figure with poise, the epitome of everything a young girl aspired to be. She wore a stunning pink taffeta prom dress with a multi-layered crinoline skirt cinched at her twenty-two-inch waist. The skirt flared out just above the knees, adding to Aunt Mary's regal allure and capturing the essence of the era's enchantment.

She was determined to teach me to dance, making me her constant partner. When I wasn't dancing with her, she twirled with the doorknob—yes, the doorknob! Inspired by her moves, I added my own flair as I shuffled across the apartment. After all, we descended from the Clubbs, a family known for writing and playing music. Music flows through our souls and rhythm dances in our feet.

. . .

Using her feminine "tactique ingénieuse," my mother secured bank loans and impeccable credit, a source of great pride throughout her life. Her financial prowess had tangible results, most notably when she splurged on a new Cadillac decked out with extravagant tail fins—an ostentatious nod to America's post-war obsession with the jet age.

As if purchased to outdo the competition, this Cadillac looked ready for liftoff! Its polished "naked lady" hubcaps and huge white wall tires turned heads everywhere we went. People did double takes when the hubcaps spun. Some concerned parents shielded their children's eyes as if our car were not suitable for children. Top down, we felt like we were in a Sunday parade, cruising with all the grandeur of a royal procession. Once home, Mommy parked that beauty in front of our front window so we could gaze at it through the glass. We had truly arrived. The sunlight was nearly blinding, causing us to temporarily forget the dark from which we emerged.

Beyond the glamour and gleaming hubcaps, the world was undergoing profound changes. Martin Luther King Jr. was arrested that year in Atlanta, and the Civil Rights Movement took on new urgency and meaning. The nation grappled with the clamor for justice and equality and struggled to catch up with the promised prosperity of our times.

That year, *To Kill a Mockingbird* was published, capturing the complexities of racial tensions in the South through the eyes of Scout Finch. Harper Lee's novel struck a communal chord, painting a picture of the stark realities of prejudice and the importance of empathy. Atticus Finch, Scout's father, became a symbol of moral integrity, standing against the tides of ignorance and hatred. The book's themes of justice, courage, and compassion resonated deeply, reflecting the very struggles the nation faced. It served as a literary beacon in a tumultuous time, underscoring the need for change and the power of standing up for what is right.

Despite the intensity of the times, balmy summer evenings felt like dreams crafted from golden light and soft breezes. Aunt Mary took me on the back of her bike, and we glided through our new neighborhood for miles. After escaping Jack's terror, life was full of unspoken magic. The world seemed to hold its breath, suspended in a moment of perfect, fleeting beauty, the air full of possibility and hope awaiting fulfillment.

But as soon as the dawn broke each morning, reality returned. My mother, always in a rush, dashed off to work. On mornings when there were no groceries at home, she handed me a few dollars and sent me to the local grocer on my way to school. I'd pick up bologna, potato chips, brown paper bags, and a loaf of bread, then set up shop at the counter next to the cash register to make sandwiches for Mary and me. The clerk watched curiously but never said a word, as if he, too, understood that this small, unspoken routine was part of our world, shaped by both dreams and necessity.

Sometimes, I fell short on funds, and the cashier noted the difference for my mother to settle over the weekend.

My sister, Mary, was a delightful rarity. She treated her "Suzy Qs"—devil's food cake sandwiches with thick white crème—as hidden treasures, tucking them away in the secret drawer of her headboard as if they were priceless artifacts. She rarely ate them; when she did, she savored the crème for hours and never gained an ounce. I sometimes found these treats months later, lumps of chocolate and sugar crème transformed into unrecognizable, calorie-laden relics.

Mary's fashion sense was as quirky as her dietary habits—she would sometimes layer clothes over her pajamas, creating a style that was uniquely her own. My mother and I would often ask, "Why, Mary?" to which she would simply grin and keep marching to the beat of her own drum.

Though she always insisted otherwise, it was clear my mother favored Mary—perhaps drawn to her pale, peaked skin, as if untouched by the sun. Her slender frame, so delicate she sometimes seemed too thin and fragile, left her looking perpetually light, almost weightless—a stark contrast to my more solid frame.

Perhaps, too, my mother saw Mary as more easily manipulated, a silent partner in bolstering her own insecurities. It seemed as though she quietly leaned on Mary to fill the gaps in her own self-image, always holding her up as the ideal, or maybe it was more than that— perhaps my mother's lingering affection for my father was partly fulfilled by Mary, who looked so much like him and shared many of his intellectual eccentricities, as if she carried forward some part of him that my mother couldn't let go.

Mary hated school. Even as early as kindergarten, she wanted to quit, and we often had to drag her along. I'm still curious what she planned to do all day. Though she hated school, Mary's curiosity knew no bounds—she wanted to try everything, even things meant for adults. She once used her cunning to get me to show her friends how to smoke a cigarette. It was a big event, a secret mission that took place in the basement. Mary brought the cigarettes, matches, and a group of eager kids and tasked me with the burden of putting on a demonstration. The kids watched intently as Mary handed me a lit cigarette. I took a puff, then tossed it to the ground and stomped on it with force. My message was clear, and no one watching ever tried smoking again, incidentally proving that Mary's mischievous ideas could lead to unexpected lessons.

My sisters and I were so proud of our bunk beds, stacked three high like a tower of childhood glory. I was on top, queen of my perch, Mary was in the middle, and baby sister Linda took the bottom bunk. It felt like a treehouse fortress, a secret hideout of sorts. One night, Aunt Mary decided to crash on the second bunk. But in her dreamy haze, she rolled off the bunk and crashed to the floor with a thud so loud it could've been heard in the next county. The room shook like we were in the middle of an earthquake. But Aunt Mary? She was fine—just a bit stunned. Meanwhile, my mother, blissfully oblivious to the whole ordeal, remained sound asleep in her full-sized bed across the room, as though nothing had happened at all.

When Aunt Mary got a job at Steak 'n Shake, I was thrilled for her.

I can still picture her wearing her black and white uniform and soda jerk paper hat. At the time, dining out was becoming a major trend. Places like Steak 'n Shake and Chuck-A-Burger became the ultimate hangouts, where the sizzle of burgers and the clink of milkshake glasses created a laid-back, cool vibe.

On weekends, we visited my grandparents. The Beatles released the sensational hits "I Wanna Hold Your Hand" and "Hey Jude." Their music energized everyone, including my grandparents in middle America, where convention typically ruled the day. Hearing talent from the UK made us feel like part of a bigger world.

It seemed the times, the stars, and the universe were perfectly aligned. People were ambitious, working hard and playing hard.

Each summer, we headed to Farmington, two hours south of St. Louis, for family gatherings with the Dickey and Clubb families. My great-grandparents lived in a small two-bedroom house in Farmington, and our get-togethers took place at their one-story white shingle bungalow.

There was a never-ending buffet of country fried chicken, mashed potatoes and gravy, collard greens, corn on the cob, and green beans. And oh, the desserts! I loved sampling everything—ambrosia and apple pies and rhubarb with ice cream. Conversations spilled out of the open kitchen window, the men gathering outside to shoot the breeze. While dinner simmered and those inviting aromas tested our patience, the women gossiped.

In a room of nearly a dozen women, there was always a subtle game of one-upmanship—boasting about children's achievements or recent encounters with acquaintances. A touch of cattiness often lingered, and my mother remained poised to showcase her latest triumphs. I remember she invariably upstaged everyone, her competitive streak shining through in her understated yet relentless way. Meanwhile, kids and others darted around the neighborhood, engaged in various games.

Evenings came alive with the rich strains of bluegrass, folklore, and the occasional hymn, accompanied by guitar, banjo, and fiddle. Grandpa Roy savored one drink after another, his Southern twang growing louder and more exuberant with each sip. As he became more inebriated, his joyful, unsteady vocal performances took over the expansive DIY concrete porch, his deep moonshine-soaked voice resonating through the neighborhood and outdoing the cicadas, katydids, and crickets. In those moments, Grandpa Roy was in his element, reveling in the music as if each drink unleashed a deep-seated yearning to love and be loved, drawing everyone onto the patio for family companionship.

During those carefree twilight hours, we chased lightning bugs and captured them in jars, wandering down the gravel and grass-covered street. Against this backdrop stood a magnificent weeping willow, its long branches swaying like a ballerina in the soft evening breeze.

On hot days, we headed to Springdale Park and its seemingly endless swimming pool that stretched out like a watery highway. The shallow end gradually deepened, leading to three dive boards at the far end, where impossibly handsome lifeguards perched like beach-bound gods. Every girl in or near the pool longed for the attention of the lifeguards—even a brief notice would suffice. The scents of outdoor picnics—ribs and burgers sizzling on the barbecue—mixed with the unmistakable scent of suntan lotion and beer. By eight in the morning, the park was packed with cars.

Every time we headed to the park, we met up with Mom's best friend, Anne, and others. We roamed freely between the pool and the concession stand, where the jukebox played non-stop. When a song grabbed us, we showed off our dance moves before heading back to the sun and water or lapping up a soft serve ice cream cone.

We delighted in the city's many treasures, from the majestic Clydesdales parading through the streets to the charming Bevo Mill, a hub for German and Czechoslovakian polka parties and Oktoberfest. Everyone from our old Hickory Street neighborhood gathered there for live polka music and dancing. I learned to polka and grew to appreciate ethnic European food.

The Veiled Prophet parade, a grand and mystical spectacle, captivated young and old. Hosted by the secretive Veiled Prophet Organization, this annual event featured lavish floats, marching bands, and elaborate costumes, all led by the enigmatic Veiled Prophet. The parade culminated in the crowning of the Veiled Prophet Queen of Love and Beauty, adding a touch of glamour to the festivities. Attending was a cherished tradition that always fit into our summer plans.

That year—the year before my father's death—was one of the most enjoyable times of my life. Amidst social upheaval and profound change was a palpable sense of awakening and possibility. The world seemed to burst with new ideas, vibrant music, and the promise of a brighter future. Every moment gushed excitement and discovery—from watching history unfold on television to dancing to the latest tunes with my family. The simple pleasures of life—learning to read with first-grade primers such as *Dick and Jane* and *Go, Dog, Go* and racing ahead of my peers in reading, writing, and arithmetic—held profound meaning. I relished quiet, loving moments with my sisters and mom. If only they lasted.

FROM MOB TIES TO MIRACLES

CHAPTER 3

ECHOES OF DECEIT: JACK'S SINISTER PATH

Everywhere we went, the shadow of Jack McCormack lingered, an unresolved presence that haunted our progress and hid behind our smiles. While we embraced the changes Jack's absence forced upon us, his specter loomed in the background, a reminder of a past we left behind.

One year after Mom claimed her independence, Jack had become a notorious convict and gang leader. His rap sheet included charges for narcotic sales, gambling, car theft, robbery, burglary, larceny, and arson. He'd been arrested numerous times since age fifteen and was under investigation by the Wellston Police in St. Louis County. Then he was arrested and booked on suspicion of first-degree murder of John Myszak, a St. Louis County real estate operator shot to death while standing in the driveway of a client's home.

It appeared that Mr. and Mrs. Myszak were having domestic difficulties, and she had sought help from Jack and John Paul Spica, conspiring with them to have her husband murdered. Spica, one of my father's associates, was also arrested for the murder.

After hours of questioning, my father was released. Myszak's widow helped the police find Spica guilty of receiving $1,000 in marked bills, implicating him in the murder. Mrs. Myszak and Spica were convicted and both served time in prison.

Jack's notoriety wasn't confined to his own actions; it extended to the dangerous circles he moved in. Spica once shared a cell block with James Earl Ray, the man convicted of murdering Dr. King. Years after Spica was released from jail, the St. Louis mobster met his grisly end via a car bombing. When he turned the key to start his car, the explosion killed him instantly and shattered windows throughout the neighborhood, a chilling reminder of the violent underworld in which he was entangled.

Spica's 1979 death occurred one year after his closed-door testimony to the House Committee regarding the murder of Reverend Martin Luther King Jr. Government officials publicly discounted any connection between Dr. King's death and the Spica car bombing; however, the documents related to his testimony remain sealed until 2027.

Among the debris of Spica's demolished Cadillac, police sources uncovered pages from an address book containing the names of Tony Giordano, James Giammanco, Paul J. Leisure, and other notorious figures from St. Louis's underbelly.

• • •

In August of 1962, headlines declared, "Gang Leader Suspect in Busch Hold Up Caught." I grabbed a copy, only to see Daddy staring back at me. The reports read:

Elmer Otto (Jack) McCormack, ex-convict, was arrested and charged with armed robbery in connection with the Anheuser Busch Credit Union heist on August 2, 1962. McCormack had masterminded the robbery, making multiple visits to the Credit Union to set up the job.

Soon after, he made bail, and my father arrived in front of our house in a gleaming, new black Cadillac—exactly the kind of extravagant vehicle we expected. He implored my mother to let him take my sisters and me out for lunch, and she relented. It had been a while since we last saw him, and despite longing for a new start with him, I was plagued with reservations. Soon, we arrived at our destination, where we collected a stunning blonde woman named Shirley.

"This is your new mother," he said in the introduction.

My heart sank. How could he do this? I felt a profound hurt, a pain that cut deep and shattered any remnants of trust that remained. I hated him at that moment and wanted to flee. He was ripping my heart into shreds, and I used every ounce of strength not to cry, to stand tall, and to keep my demeanor unchanged, refusing to let my anguish show. At just eight years old, I marshaled control over my insides and put on a cordial, superficial sweetness, trying to appear a proper little girl.

Once he impressed Shirley with his supposed stability and attractiveness as a caring father, he returned us home to my mother. He was too busy for us, and we had already served our purpose.

The Anheuser Busch robbery was later deemed an inside job. Jack conspired with a woman who worked at the credit union. For many years, I surmised Shirley was that woman and suspected this was their first of many planned bank robberies.

Earlier that year, he was charged with stealing two cars. He was also the suspected ringleader of a crew that stole and dismantled cars, then sold the parts at a salvage yard. This thieving method was more profitable and harder to trace than selling the cars whole. Components like doors, fenders, roofs, and hoods were sold in large quantities and brought in large amounts of cash.

The credit union robbery was executed by two men armed with pistols who escaped in a car driven by a third accomplice. One of the suspects removed the license plate and threw it down a manhole, foolishly thinking the move ensured the perfect crime. As fate would have it, a bystander saw it all and reported it to the police. All the authorities needed was to recover the plates and find the registered owner. Even with a criminal mastermind at work, crime never pays.

Rumor had it that Jack, just thirty-seven years old, received most of the money from the credit union robbery. Wherever the money went, it was never recovered. He insisted he was innocent and had his cover firmly in place. My father still lived on Cranberry Lane, a couple of years after my mother and we had moved out, and claimed to be a salesman.

When the news broke about my father's involvement in the robbery, the buzz among family and friends was deafening. It was clear that this was the "big deal" Daddy had boasted about, and suddenly, everyone who knew him felt the need to distance themselves, fearing his misdeeds might cast a shadow on them.

The community was awash with speculation. Neighbors and relatives endlessly debated where the stolen money was hidden, each person concocting their own theories. Amidst the chatter, one thing was certain—my mother had no clue where the cash was hidden or any desire to know its location.

My father's arrest and his vehement denial of involvement only fueled the rumors. Although he was granted bail and released—thanks to his cunning and cleverness, which kept him rarely convicted and always just out of reach—our worry grew heavier. His tangled web of deceit, involving stolen cars and now the credit union heist, were closing in on him. A sense of impending doom was unmistakable; it became increasingly clear that the consequences of his actions were catching up with him, and his escape from the inevitable seemed more improbable with each passing day.

CHAPTER 4

THE HELPLESS CRY OF GOODBYE: THE MURDER OF MY FATHER AND MY FAREWELL

ON THE EVENING OF SATURDAY, OCTOBER 26, 1962, MY two sisters and I were with our great-aunt Frances Rickert. She was a plump, elderly woman with a fondness for my father, often playfully flirting with and teasing Daddy with a sparkle in her eye. Frances lived in a modest one-bedroom flat near our apartment. That weekend, my mother craved a restful evening out and offered Frances a few bucks to babysit us.

Aunt Frances was famously frugal, providing us just one sheet of toilet paper at a time. "You little girls only need one tissue," she declared. My sisters and I collapsed into giggles, transforming her stern rationing into a playful rebellion we dubbed the "Hanky-Spanky Toilet Paper Holdup." "Better make this one last," I said through giggles, "or we'll be stuck with corncobs!" We concocted wild, imaginative scenarios, dreaming up clever alternatives to TP. The cramped bathroom became our little stage, where we pretended to rival Frances's authority with impish defiance. Who knew something as ordinary as toilet paper could spark such gleeful mischief?

The atmosphere that evening was as tranquil as a serene countryside at dusk. Frances sat comfortably in her easy chair, the television on the local news at low volume. Mary, Linda, and I took turns gently brushing Aunt Frances's soft, gray hair, creating a soothing rhythm that lowered Aunt Frances's blood pressure with every stroke. With the peaceful simplicity of the moment and the TV's hushed tones, it felt like time slowed down. It was a tranquil and cherished moment, the calm before a storm.

Then the storm arrived. Like an unexpected lightning bolt splitting the night sky, I heard a familiar name: "Jack McCormack." The announcer's voice was stern, commanding the attention of my sisters, great-aunt, and me. His tone made it clear that this was significant news, and I needed to pay attention.

Even in the largest crowd, the mention of your surname—especially "Jack McCormack"—triggered a primal response, a fight-or-flight instinct. This time was no different.

I spun toward Aunt Frances's small black-and-white television and watched as men guided a stretcher toward the coroner's vehicle. A white sheet covered the stretcher, hiding the man beneath it—my father. My head spun. My world quaked. It felt like waking from a dream, a haze of disbelief clouding my mind.

"Jack McCormack, ex-convict," the announcer continued, "the reputed 'brains' of the Anheuser Busch Credit Union robbery, has just been fatally shot."

It wasn't a nightmare; it was real. The realization hit me like a sledgehammer.

Aunt Frances held a hand over her mouth in disbelief and hastened to the black rotary telephone on the vanity. In a flurry, she dialed my grandmother. I listened in a stupor, as Aunt Frances confirmed that yes—Daddy was murdered.

Disbelief washed over me as time came to an abrupt stop. Uncertainty swirled. Mixed emotions coursed through me. I wanted to believe this was a bad movie, a nightmare I would soon wake from. There would be no waking from this nightmare.

Once again, Jack left the way he always did—with a sharp thud to the hearts, no goodbye, just the heavy silence of absence. My mother was beside herself. Despite moving on without him, she clung to the hope that my father would one day change his ways. Though separated, they were not divorced; that lingering hope became a bitter, unfinished story.

At just thirty-seven years old, Daddy was gone too soon. Words left unsaid and actions left undone would never have a chance to be said or done. No more opportunities to see my father or for him to change his ways, to be the man God had intended him to be. It was too soon, and there were many regrets. My lost and emotionally troubled Daddy never learned to love properly, live honorably, change his course, and let us love him as we so wanted.

While we grieved and went through the motions of life, Winnie consoled us. A fine gentleman from my father's side of the family, Winnie brought a beautiful doll for each of us girls, and I treasured his gifts of time and care. I wished he would stay with us forever; we desperately needed him or someone like him to care for us.

Buster Wortman, the famous mobster, also reached out to my mother after Daddy's death. We went to Buster's home, where we felt a sense of family loyalty and comfort. He offered us a reassuring promise, saying to my mother, "If you ever need anything, let me know."

• • •

I'm not sure which was more emotionally difficult: learning of my father's tragic death on the evening news or sitting through his funeral. I stood in a room awash with an unsettling green Kodachrome glow, lights dimmed. The room featured a large, open casket with brass stationary bars, surrounded by an extraordinary funeral spray of white roses. The rose's intense, pungent perfume enveloped everything, mingling with the somber reality of Daddy's death laid out before me.

My mother brought the Bible home from the service, a single white rose poking out from between the pages. For years afterward, I hated the smell of roses, fearful the fragrance might resurrect a deep childhood memory. As a young woman sampling fragrances at the Saks Fifth Avenue counter, I later made peace with roses. They are now my favorite flower and fragrance.

The funeral parlor filled with the sound of hard shoes moving deliberately and slowly on hollow wood floors, punctuated by occasional whispers from attendees. I was emotionally detached, removed from those present. Loneliness and isolation gripped me tightly, threatening to unravel my tenuous composure. My resolve nearly shattered when Mommy approached the casket and, in an overwhelming display of grief, collapsed to her knees.

Anne, who was a good friend and always there for my mother, tried to lighten the mood with one of her typically misguided jokes, but her humor fell flat, profoundly misplaced amidst our collective grief. I hated her lack of decorum. A wave of desperation and disbelief crashed over me as I gripped the situation with every bit of strength I had. I feared that if I let go, I would lose all control. "I'm not here," I kept telling myself. "This is just a movie, and it will soon be over."

I longed for time to pass, but it stood still. All I could do was repeat those words over and over, clinging to them as if they might somehow make the reality of the moment fade.

At just eight years old, the weight of it all was more than I could bear. When the visitation and formalities came to an end, my mother took my hand, and we walked out, truly closing that chapter of our lives. As we stepped into the fresh air, leaving the suffocating grief behind, I could breathe again. How many years had I held my breath? And now, we reached the end of a time—a painful, turbulent era—and began the long journey toward healing.

In the days that followed, the tears flowed freely. We allowed ourselves to cry as long and as hard as we needed. I didn't return to school, missing my entire second grade year. My studies were deeply affected, another victim crushed under the weight of our loss.

A grand jury soon considered evidence against Louis Wallach for the fatal shooting of my father. As a child, I knew him as Daddy, the figure of my affection and the center of our world. But as an adult, seeing him through a more critical lens, I refer to him as Jack, no longer clinging to the innocence of the past. Wallach, a former boxing promoter and auto salvage yard owner, admitted to shooting Jack at his yard, claiming it was self-defense. However, the coroner ruled Jack's death a homicide, noting that he had been shot four times, one bullet passing through his wrist, suggesting he raised his hands in defense.

The two men had a long history of business dealings in auto parts, with Jack often visiting Wallach's salvage yard. Wallach claimed their final meeting took a different turn, alleging Jack attempted a holdup. Yet, the circumstances surrounding Jack's death raised many questions. He had spoken with police just 30 minutes before he died, and his car was found at the scene with the engine off and no keys, adding to the mystery. Police later discovered thousands of dollars' worth of stolen auto parts at Wallach's yard.

Wallach's story evolved during the trial. A September 18, 1963, *St. Louis Post-Dispatch* article reported that Wallach predicted he would shoot a "holdup man" the night before Jack's death, even showing the revolver later identified as the murder weapon. Detective Jon Becker, who had known Wallach for three years prior to the murder, testified that Wallach mentioned a "crazy man" trying to get him, referring to Jack.

Despite their complicated relationship, Wallach had told Jack to stay away from his home just days before the incident, but Jack ignored the warning. Wallach was initially found guilty, but after an appeal, he was acquitted. This tragic chapter of my life remains a haunting memory.

My mother, feeling the weight of her children's pain, sided with the defense, not wanting Wallach's children to lose their father. Years later, my sister Mary, now a real estate investor, encountered Wallach again—this time he was city inspector overseeing one of Mary's property transactions. Recognizing Wallach's name, Mary asked if he knew Jack McCormack. When he turned to her in shock, she revealed, "Well, I'm Mary McCormack. Jack was my father." It was a tense and fateful exchange that Mary struggled to process for years.

I remember little from the months that followed my father's death. The outcome of the Louis Wallach trial left me unfazed. His conviction and subsequent acquittal simply marked the time, punctuating that period of my life like the final curtain on someone else's story.

· · ·

In the summer of 1963, Uncle Billy Joe was discharged a year early from the army for medical reasons. While my mother was a consummate fighter who never gave up and considered a challenge a call to conquer, Billy wasn't blessed with resilience. He was the runt, the black sheep of the family.

When Uncle Billy returned from Vietnam, he was more troubled than before. He lacked social norms and pestered relentlessly, as if haunted by evil spirits.

Tormented in his early years by my grandparents, he became their scapegoat, subjected to ongoing abuse until he grew calloused and immune to pain. His only comfort seemed to come from making others uncomfortable, which turned his visits into dreaded nuisances.

Brimming with low self-esteem, Uncle Billy Joe was loathsome and obnoxious, a loose cannon ready to explode. However, he was only twenty-one, so we all assumed his foolishness was a phase. Sure enough, he met a girl, started dressing sharply and walking with confidence, and we thought he might be on the right track.

But a year after Daddy's death, on another ill-fated October day, we got the news that Billy Joe shot himself. Devastated by their loss, my grandparents sank into a deep depression. Watching these two unstoppable forces become subdued was heart-wrenching and surreal. Despite their torment and questionable parenting of Uncle Billy, they loved their son.

Uncle Larry and his wife, Carol, were first to know of Billy's suicide, as they spent the night in the room right next to him. When they woke up, Billy was unconscious. They called the police, only to discover Uncle Billy died hours earlier. Oddly, they claimed to sleep through the sound of a gunshot in the room next door. They were never charged with any crime.

Knowing the three of them, it wouldn't surprise me if they were playing Russian Roulette or got into a heated, alcohol-fueled argument the night before. My grandmother, Nana, never stopped speculating. She was obsessed with finding out what really happened. On visits to her house, she resorted to unseen assistance, begging us to play Ouija in hopes of getting answers. Communicating with the spirit world was Nana's go-to when this side of life got too tough. We'd dim the lights, gather around the table, and eagerly wait for some supernatural insight.

Underneath our fingertips, the planchette would move "freely" across the board. "Who killed Billy Joe?" Nana asked. "What happened to Billy?" To our amazement, the planchette spelled out one word after another. As the planchette moved, Nana buzzed with excitement, sure that her quest for answers would soon be fulfilled.

Mary, Linda, and I sat, wide-eyed, as the planchette spelled out vague messages. It seemed an innocent game, an opportunity for bonding with Nana as she sought closure. Though we never got Nana's sought-after answers, the ritual was cathartic for her, and we cherished those eerie moments together.

• • •

The same year we mourned the loss of my father, Martin Luther King Jr. delivered his iconic "I Have a Dream" speech during the March on Washington, a pivotal moment credited with helping to pass the Civil Rights Act of 1964. A year after this speech, the Ku Klux Klan bombed a Baptist church in Birmingham, Alabama, a tragic event that shocked the nation. In the background, Robert F. Kennedy made significant strides in his fight against organized crime, challenging the mob's power and corruption and further reshaping the turbulent landscape of the time.

When I returned to school at Monroe Elementary, I was excited about learning. One of our regular activities was to practice our ability to "Duck and Cover." This drill was a response to the ever-present threat of nuclear war during the Cold War era. We dropped to the ground and took cover under our desks, shielding our heads with our hands, assuming this simple act could protect us from a nuclear blast. It felt like a game at times, but there was an underlying tension that even we, as children, could sense.

At home, we watched President John F. Kennedy and his brother Robert F. Kennedy on television. I was captivated by their distinct Boston accents and the intensity with which they spoke.

There was something magnetic about their speech—so full of conviction and energy. Robert Kennedy took a particularly hard stance against organized crime, working tirelessly as attorney general to combat the mob's influence. Every time I watched them, I wanted to be right there, cheering on the Kennedy brothers. I was drawn to their cause at eight years old, eager to be a part of their world.

On Friday, November 22, 1963, I was in school when I learned about the assassination of John F. Kennedy. The announcement was brief, the weight of it settling on the room like a heavy fog. Teachers struggled to maintain their composure, while students, too young to grasp the magnitude of the event, sensed a profound shift in the air. The sadness in my heart never seemed to abate. I felt as though life was an endless battle for a modicum of peace and joy.

The nation, like our classroom, plunged into shock and mourning. Families gathered around their television sets, watching the endless news coverage, trying to make sense of what happened. A piece of hope had torn away, leaving a void that would never be filled. For many, this was the first time experiencing loss on such a grand scale. Marvin Gaye's "What's Going On" matched my inner turmoil and became an anthem for my growing sense of disillusionment over those turbulent, tragic times.

Following so much loss and heartache, 1964 brought a glimmer of hope, a sense that maybe, just maybe, things could get better. It wasn't just the world trying to heal—it was me, too. The small victories, like the passing of the Civil Rights Act, gave the nation a reason to believe there was still good to be found in the midst of all the pain. It was as if the world was offering a hand to pull me up from the depths, and I was ready to grasp it.

After so much hardship, joy and peace eventually found their way back, bringing a sense of heaven on earth. This cycle, I've since learned, is a deeply human experience—it's why we hold on to hope during tough times. It's a testament to the power of patience and perseverance, which ultimately reward us with moments of pure, unfiltered bliss.

My mother, after a year of persistent grief, found her way back to happiness. Unwilling to let the weight of the world crush her spirit, she faced every challenge with passionate abandon and took a giant leap forward, securing a job as a secretary.

With a regular paycheck, she dreamed again. One day, as she scanned the newspaper, her eyes caught a small ad:

Ranch, Breezeway, Garage, Lot 125 x 129 $400 Dn, FHA
8803 Bangert. 8 years old, radiant gas heat; tile bath; SHADE TREES, CORNER LOT.

Anticipation bubbled inside us all the way to the house, and it was love at first sight. The lovely redwood-sided ranch was on a corner lot, with a stone garden perfectly positioned at the corner. This spot, which we later called "the pond," became our designated meeting place after school. Added bonus: the fenced-in backyard meant we could have a dog once again!

The neighborhood was full of school-aged children, and an easy walk to school took us through a beautiful park. The house had two bedrooms, one bath, and a breezeway enclosed with jalousie windows.

Mom combined her social security widow benefits and savings for the $400 down payment and secured a mortgage for the remaining $8,000. A new house—what could be more exhilarating?

This was a picture of promise—our very own slice of heaven.

Once enrolled in school, we met all the neighborhood kids, including Jerry Jean, who became my best friend. With three siblings and dear friends for each of us, I rode my bike for miles. Our torturous start transformed into a perfect, carefree childhood, filled with endless possibility and boundless joy.

The summer of '64, Aunt Mary introduced my mother to a young man who initially showed interest in my aunt. It quickly became clear that they weren't meant for each other, but Aunt Mary hoped for a different outcome with my mother. Perhaps Aunt Mary sensed something special, a spark that might ignite my mother. The young man was only twenty-one, and when they met, it was like magic. He fell head over heels, and it was impossible not to notice. The way he looked at her, the breathless excitement that overtook him when they were together—he could hardly contain his passion.

My mother, nine years older and far more experienced, played it cool. She concealed her feelings with deliberate care, revealing her affection in measured doses, savoring every moment of the chase. It was thrilling to watch them, a dance in which every step was carefully choreographed yet bursting with emotion.

They were truly in love, two souls who seemed destined for one another against the odds. Together, they became better versions of themselves, bringing out the best in each other. Such a union is rare and beautiful—a divinely orchestrated relationship that embodied everything marriage was meant to be.

He was eager to make this wonderful woman with three children, living in the suburbs, his own. Not long after, he proposed, and they decided to tie the knot on Christmas Eve. I still remember the day he and Mom announced the big news. "Kids," she said, "we're going to get married. Wayne wants to be your dad."

Our hearts swelled with overwhelming joy, a deep, unspoken longing that filled every corner of our being. It was a joy that transcended the moment, lingering in our souls and leaving us yearning for more.

"Can we call you Daddy?" we asked over and over. We had dreamed for our whole lives—a father to have all to ourselves. We repeated his new name over and over, savoring the sound of it, as if saying it enough times would make it real. Having a "Daddy" of our own was the missing piece of our family puzzle, fulfilling our deepest desire for a real dad.

Wayne answered the call. It was as if he'd waited his whole life to step into the role of husband and father, and now that it was within his grasp, he embraced it with everything he had. He wanted to shoulder the responsibility of caring for us, to be the man upon whom we could depend. He cherished this calling deeply. I remember him putting on the music from *West Side Story*. He was particularly moved by "Maria" and "There's a Place for Us," songs that seemed to tap into the most tender, vulnerable part of his soul—the part that craved an endless, all-consuming love.

Once while we listened to *West Side Story*, Wayne laced up a pair of roller skates and glided back and forth through the living room, reveling in his fresh ecstasy. It was a sight to behold—a grown man, head over heels in love, skating around like a kid at a roller rink. He was perfect for my mother, who, in her own way, was a child at heart. She adored his innocence and his genuine, authentic vulnerability. He was exactly what we needed. He had all the ambition and drive of a young man who had fallen hard for his new, ready-made family and embraced his role as provider, loving father, and passionate husband.

Their passion? Based on the red and gold medallion wallpaper and matching, tufted red and gold bedspread, it must have been intense. It was a bit awkward when family and friends commented on the, um, "bold" decor. Looking back, it's clear my mother, who always seemed prim and proper, had something going on in that bedroom—because my new sister, Regina Darice, made her debut shortly thereafter!

FROM MOB TIES TO MIRACLES

CHAPTER 5

CONDOMS, CRUSHES, AND THE GREAT BUBBLE BATH DEBACLE: AN AMERICAN DREAM GONE AWRY

IF YOU'VE EVER WATCHED "SPRINGTIME FOR HITLER" FROM *The Producers*, you'll understand the surreal, almost satirical essence that encapsulated my parents' lives. Imagine this: my mother and stepfather, wildly ambitious and brimming with the most outlandish ideas in the name of success, as if they were actors in some kabuki theater of high-stakes schemes. There was no venture too harebrained, no plan too audacious for them to try. I swear, all those flaming ideas were cooked up in that red bedroom—where else could such a storm of ambition possibly take root?

Wayne, young and full of energy, was the "concrete guy," holding a reservoir of ambition that defied logic. Meanwhile, my mother was the mad scientist operating behind the scenes, the architect of every scheme. It was the perfect marriage of dreams and implementation— one devising elaborate plans, the other trying to make them reality. Truly, the pair knew no bounds.

Wayne did well selling pharmaceuticals, but after spending far too many hours in doctors' waiting rooms, he decided it was time for a change. And what better way to venture into new territory than with a bold, entrepreneurial spirit? Wayne always said you could never get rich working for someone, so he and Mom became fearless entrepreneurs. They dove headfirst into bubble bath manufacturing, convinced it was the next big thing. The house soon transformed into a bubble bath factory, with mountains of pink and blue containers filled with lilac, rose, oriental, and bergamot-scented bubbles stashed in every corner. We essentially lived inside a French bubble bath factory. The only thing missing was success.

As luxurious as our bathroom smelled, those bubbles didn't translate into cash flow. Undeterred, my parents pivoted again—this time into the glamorous world of wiglets. Yep, mini wigs. They even did TV commercials, trying to sell hairpieces to the masses, but once again, their big idea didn't take off. Their entrepreneurial spirit was impressive, even if the business ideas floated like a bain moussant in the wind.

Once wiglets flopped, Wayne started schlepping pantyhose like a man on a mission, leaving my mother at home knee-deep in ribbon and fabric, making what she swore were "exquisite" lampshades. Mom hunted down and used every shade and style of ribbon under the sun—braided, twisted, bedazzled—to embellish her shades. In the end, her supposed masterpieces were over-the-top, Victorian-meets-Liberace excess.

While Dad stocked shelves with the latest pantyhose options, Mom scratched her head, trying to figure out why the world wasn't ready for her artistic vision. With deep affection and admiration, I must say, she never gave up.

Fortunately, the Legg Pantyhose line was raking in the dough, with Dad—I took to calling Wayne this familiar name—making serious strides into grocery stores across St. Louis and St. Louis County. He had his fingers in every hosiery pie in town, picking up closeouts and flipping them to grocers like a hosiery hustler.

Then Mary—my maverick sister—started working for Wayne. She was sixteen, fierce, and ready to take on the world—or, more specifically, our stepdad.

Mary wasn't just another teen trying to sell pantyhose; she was out to beat Wayne at his own game. She hit the road with all the ambition of a seasoned pro, determined to outsell, outshine, and outdo him in every way.

Her determination to outshine Dad often led to amusing situations. During a meeting with an in-store buyer, Mary exuded confidence, fully embodying the role of a sharp, young businesswoman. She confidently grabbed an iconic egg-shaped container of Leggs pantyhose, believing it contained the sought-after hosiery. The innovative packaging, celebrated for its eye-catching design and retail appeal, was a marketing breakthrough of its era. However, under the pressure of navigating my dad's box of closeout items, identifying the right product wasn't always as effortless as it seemed.

She held it up proudly, practically dazzling the room with her sales pitch, when horror struck.

The box of hosiery didn't have a single pair of pantyhose. Poor Mary looked at her hand and realized she wasn't holding pantyhose, toys, or anything remotely related to the family business. Nope, this was a whole other kind of protection. Instead of hose, Mary was waving around a box of condoms like it was the best deal in town. Her face turned fifty shades of red as the awkwardness of the situation hit her like a freight train.

We laughed about that for years, and Dad never let her forget it.

Dad wasn't just hustling pantyhose—he and my mother had quite the enterprise going. Alongside hosiery, they started selling furniture. At one point, our basement was crammed full of Flexsteel sofas, each more beautiful than the last. Not content with just selling, my parents eventually tried their hand at manufacturing. They bought wholesale frames, upholstery fabric, and trim, and began building furniture from scratch.

With every venture, Mom and Dad sharpened their business instincts and honed their taste for finer goods. They weren't happy with mediocrity; they longed to offer the best of everything—quality was king. Professionalism didn't come naturally, though. Their success came from sheer grit, determination, and the willingness to evolve, refining their business and business sense every step of the way.

Every spring, our family piled into the car and headed to Chicago for the Housewares Trade Show at McCormick Place. There, over 50,000 wholesalers, retailers, and manufacturers from all corners of the country (and some from overseas) showcasing their latest products. The long concrete aisles stretched on forever, filled with vendors offering everything from award-winning kitchen gadgets to the latest in home décor.

My father scoured booths, searching for merchandise to pitch to grocery store clients in St. Louis. I loved every minute of it—the glamour of commerce, the energy in the air, the sense of possibility. It felt like we were part of something bigger, and it was an honor to bring a piece of that excitement back to St. Louis to fuel our family enterprise.

They seemed destined for success, however, and their hard work started to get noticed by friends and family. Both my parents were workaholics, absorbed in their ventures. My mother often said, "The harder we work, the luckier we get."

In the 1960s, this was all part of the American Dream—a *Leave It to Beaver* story playing out in households across the country. For those chasing their slice of heaven, it was a race to glory.

• • •

Neither of my parents had the slightest clue about running a business when they first started, but they were determined to self-educate, no matter what it took. When Mom needed to write a letter but had no idea how to begin, she rummaged through every letter she ever received, picking out the best phrases and reworking them into her own version of a professional boilerplate. It was trial and error at its finest.

Marketing? Business strategies? Business ethics? Analytics? Economics? Operations? Budgets? Taxes? Communication? Mom and Dad didn't know the first thing about any of it. But they learned fast. Every misstep became a lesson, and every success fueled their hunger for more. They were relentless, figuring things out piece by piece, determined to build something bigger than their limitations.

Wayne's determination came into clearer focus late at night when the house was quiet, after everyone else went to bed. He sat at his old, beat-up, heavy maple desk, worn from years of use. To his right sat an electric, manual adding machine, its tape roll ready for action.

Sometimes, he let me stay up past bedtime and sit with him. I'd watch him hunch over for hours, fingers tirelessly working the keys, feeding the machine numbers until every calculation was accounted for with absolute precision. The rhythm of the machine, the steady clicking and whirring, echoed the persistence that defined Dad. Every time he reviewed the tape revealed a sense of purpose, a relentless drive to get it right. The tactile connection between his hands and the machine represented a small victory—each number a step closer to the dream.

There was something rewarding in the routine, an almost meditative focus that kept Dad going night after night. His work ethic was woven into every inch of that desk and every inch of his soul.

That same relentless passion and focus took hold of me when I met Mrs. Nemisch, my third-grade music teacher. A true enchantress, Mrs. Nemisch was Russian. She had perfectly groomed charcoal hair and a finely sculpted nose. Her accent held mystery, and her knowledge of the classics captivated me. She played the piano beautifully. Through her, I was introduced to Beethoven, Ravel, Bach, and Schubert—names that soon became my companions in a world of music.

I sat entranced, allowing these artists' masterpieces to envelop my mind, spiraling into dreams of orchestras and grand symphonies. I learned to tune my ear to each distinct note—the piano's delicate keys, the bold call of the horns, the precise rhythm of the percussion, the violins' soulful strings—all fighting to captivate the listener's heart. Those melodies sparked an electricity that coursed through my being. After school, I envisioned myself standing before an audience, baton in hand, commanding a full orchestra. I heard every measure, each note suspended in the air, savoring every nuance as if I were already there, leading the orchestra toward a magnificent crescendo.

Mrs. Nemisch opened a door into a world I hadn't known existed, and my imagination was dazzled. I'm still grateful to her for igniting that love of music within me. I couldn't get enough then, and I still can't.

And then there was Mr. Long—my sixth-grade teacher, my favorite teacher of all time, and my first real crush. He was so handsome, and I always tried to sit next to him at the lunch table. In my young eyes, he was "the" guy. Beyond his looks, Mr. Long had an incredible ability to teach. He came up with the cleverest strategies for helping us learn math and English, and I was determined to be his best student. But being painfully shy made it difficult to stand out in class or win any kind of popularity contest. Looking back, I realize that striving for attention was a waste of energy. It wasn't in my nature to be the life of the party or the most popular kid in class, and no amount of effort could change that. Trying to be something I wasn't was counterproductive, but my admiration for Mr. Long—and the way he made learning exciting— still sticks with me.

One of Mr. Long's brilliant ideas was using stats from the Cardinals baseball team for class assignments. We'd have to calculate everything from batting averages to earned run averages, strikeout ratios, and winning percentages. For me, it was game on. I ran those numbers in my head and finished well before my classmates got through the first column. Every time I finished first, it was like hitting a home run. Score! Yes! I was becoming the class scholar—genius, even—and Mr. Long took notice. It felt like I was finally standing out, like I'd cracked the code to getting his attention.

Halfway through the school year, I burned through all of Mr. Long's assignments. He was running out of ideas to keep me busy, so he created something special just for me and Colleen McHenry. He called it the "Independence Group." In theory, we were both at the head of the class, but there was one problem: Colleen sat behind me. And trust me, she was always on my radar.

Colleen McHenry wasn't just the class beauty—oh no, she was the full package. Beautiful and smart. I was determined not to let her upstage me, ever. Colleen's mother was a hairdresser, which explained why Colleen always looked like she'd just stepped out of a salon. Every day, she waltzed into class with her hair perfectly teased into a neat little flip at the ends, frozen in place with hairspray. It was flawless. She wore a subtle, elegant perfume—likely a selection made just for her at the fragrance counter of Famous Barr—while I sat there in my sweaty cardigans, feeling like I carried the scent of erasers and textbooks.

One day, Colleen showed up with her hair a bit lighter, like she'd gotten it freshly highlighted. There it was—every strand in its perfect place, gleaming under the fluorescent lights. The best part? It didn't move. Not during kickball, not during recess, not ever. It was like she'd mastered the art of frozen hair. Meanwhile, the rest of us were sweating and gasping for air while Colleen remained an untouched porcelain doll.

But wait, there's more! A week later, Colleen showed up to school with her hair transformed into a dazzling bleached blonde, channeling full Marilyn Monroe vibes!

Naturally, this was an instant hit with the boys. It was like she waved a magic wand and suddenly every boy in class was fawning over her. I couldn't help but wonder, after she had her pick, if there might be one left over for me. Just one, maybe?

There I sat in front of Colleen with her perfectly coiffed hair, her matching outfits, and those darling Mary Jane shoes. We were most definitely aware of each other, but we each pretended the other did not exist, as if we were locked in some silent, unspoken rivalry. She had her hair; I had my math scores. And so, the battle continued.

But I had the upper hand. Mr. Long was my type. He loved math, adored the St. Louis Cardinals, and clearly favored me. When it came time for the final school spelling bee, he gave me hints to secure the win. But when it became a contest between him and me, I was unyielding. Stubborn as ever, I'd insist on doing things my way, even if it meant losing. That was my line in the sand. And, truth be told, I didn't like his cologne either. It's silly, but I can still remember the smell, which was oddly reminiscent of celery.

Mr. Long was single, but to my dismay, he began spending time with the new art teacher. (Her name escapes me—probably because I'm still bitter.) They started seeing each other, and I couldn't wrap my head around it. Her? Over me? I mean, sure, she had a foot in height on me and maybe a bit more sophistication, but really? I was so mad at Mr. Long. I gave him attitude every chance I got—though I doubt he ever noticed.

On the bright side, while I was busy being mad at Mr. Long, someone else started paying attention: Tommy Larkin. He was beginning to take notice, and let's just say that was enough to make me forget about Mr. Long's questionable cologne.

And speaking of things that could never be forgotten—let's talk Cardinals baseball. The St. Louis Cardinals rocked! Especially in 1964, when they won the World Series at Busch Stadium, the pride of August Busch himself.

There was nothing quite like following the games and listening to the iconic voices of Harry Caray and Jack Buck on the radio. Their deep, jovial, smiling voices were part of the magic woven into the fabric of my childhood. To this day, their voices still echo in my mind, reminding me of that rich and colorful past.

• • •

Summers at our house were always lively, with my parents throwing backyard parties. Yard games were a staple of these gatherings, while inside, my mother and I were hard at work, setting the table and preparing a savory feast. It was a routine we perfected—entertainment outside, labor inside. But not everything about those gatherings was routine.

Enter Aunt Mary, always dressed to make a statement. In her short shorts and low-cut blouse, she'd saunter over to my stepfather and challenge him to a game of croquet. It was innocent, on the surface. But there was something about the way she played that game, the way she'd lean just a bit too far over the mallet or laugh too loudly at something Wayne said. My mother would peer out the kitchen window, pausing mid-preparation to take it all in, her expression tightening as Aunt Mary flirted openly with Wayne.

They seemed to have way too much fun, and the more I watched, the more I noticed how Mary's actions felt deliberate—each teasing gesture a little bolder than the last. It was off-color for sure, but no one addressed it. Instead, we tucked it away, filed under "things best left unsaid," tagging it as one of those peculiar moments that lingered in the corners of our memories, waiting for a time when they might be reconsidered in a different light.

•••

As my parents climbed the social ladder, others in the family did not. There was blatant jealousy among those left behind, and it didn't help that my mother, with her natural competitive streak, never missed an opportunity to flaunt their achievements. She had this way of dropping little comments designed to remind others just how far they'd come.

One of her favorite lines was, "Wayne and I have the perfect marriage—he likes to make money, and I like to spend it." She'd say it with a smile, as if it were a playful remark, but the underlying edge. It was her way of letting everyone know they'd made it, and she wasn't shy about rubbing it in.

Though both my father and stepfather lost their parents before reaching adulthood, leaving them to navigate life alone, my stepfather found warmth and stability in his close relationship with his grandparents, especially his beloved grandmother, Elsie McAuliffe. Her kindness created a special bond for us both, offering a sense of family love that bridged the loss.

Elsie and I hit it off immediately. We both wore the same size four, which added to our connection. She lived in a stunning urban apartment with elegant furnishings that exuded understated luxury. Her taste was impeccable—blue and beige ensembles paired with discreet, sophisticated decor. Quiet elegance was all about her. Everything from her muted styles to her graceful demeanor drew me in. It was so refreshing, especially compared to my mother's affinity for bright reds and oranges.

One week after our first visit to meet Elsie, to my surprise, I received a package from her. Inside were several of her sheath dresses—hardly worn, in all the beautiful, muted colors I admired. The fit was like a glove, and it was the first time I truly felt like a young lady. My mother, recognizing this new transformation, bought me my first pair of high heels. I was ready to show the world my new look, thanks to Elsie.

• • •

My parents were always hard workers, but as their success grew, they started taking us to church every Sunday, as if sensing that there was something more important to life than climbing the social ladder. One Sunday evening, we attended a special service to hear a traveling evangelist named Vincent Constantino. He wasn't like the preachers I was used to—his words were simple, yet they held a power that resonated deeply within me.

As he explained the story of salvation and what Jesus did at Calvary, it wasn't just the biblical account that captured my attention—it was the underlying message about what it meant to be human, to endure life's highs and lows. His words awoke something in me, a sense that there was more to life than the material success my parents chased. He presented life as a search for meaning, one that went beyond ambition, beyond the worldly measures of accomplishment. For the first time, I felt the stirring of something I couldn't quite name, but it was profound and lasting.

Years later, a colleague suggested that perhaps my faith was just a crutch—a way to get by in life. But I knew that wasn't true. What Vincent Constantino sparked in me that night was far more than a way to cope. It gave me a foundation to explore the deeper questions of existence, to search for meaning in every moment. That hour, at nearly thirteen years old, marked the beginning of a lifelong journey—a search for understanding, for wisdom, for the heart of what it means to truly live.

The philosophical depth that came from that simple sermon wasn't about seeking external validation; it was the beginning of a conscious awakening to life's mysteries. This realization has shaped me ever since, guiding me through life's ups and downs, and reminding me that there's always something deeper to seek beyond the surface and the obvious markers of success.

. . .

In contrast, my relationship with Jerry Jean, my best friend, wasn't born out of some grand design but rather out of proximity. Life didn't hand me the perfect family or friends, but sometimes convenience is its own kind of blessing. Jerry Jean lived just across the street, and while she was closer in age and more mentally aligned with my sister Mary, she and I found our own rhythm together. Academically, she wasn't the fastest, but her sincerity made up for it, cementing our friendship in a way that went beyond intellect.

We spent hours playing board games, especially Monopoly, games stretching on for weeks. The excitement never waned, no matter how long we played. One pivotal moment served as a personal test of honesty. We were nearing the end of a game, and I was a hair away from losing. The temptation to rearrange the board while we stepped away for dinner was strong—no one would have known. But as I wrestled with the idea, I realized that winning through deceit would make me a loser in my own eyes. In that moment, I made a personal commitment to honesty, trusting that fate would take care of the rest.

Jerry Jean wasn't much for outdoor adventures, but our sleepovers were a blast. At our house, thanks to my father's grocery business, dinner often meant steak from our fully stocked freezer—a treat that made our sleepovers with Jerry Jean feel extra special. But when we went to her place, her mother served up an entirely different exprerience with unusual salads and delightful entrees, adding a touch of creativity and variety to our meals. Weekend sleepovers were a little escape from the world. We set up makeshift beds on the floor, talked about the silliest things, and snacked until we couldn't move anymore. Those were the best kind of nights.

Homework sessions became a regular thing too, and we always managed to do Jerry Jean's first. There was something special about those moments—maybe it was the simplicity of it all, or the way our friendship had its quirks and dynamics. Whatever it was, those sleepovers weren't just fun—they were a kind of youthful magic that made life feel lighter, full of possibility. And even though we were different in many ways, our bond felt just right, imperfect as it was.

I remember our conversation after Jerry Jean's first kiss. She was ahead of me in that department, and naturally, my curious sister Mary had to know every detail. "So, Jerry Jean, how long did it last?" she pried. Mary, always the instigator, began counting seconds out loud: "One . . . two . . . three . . . four . . ." Jerry, looking pleased with herself, chimed in around five seconds. At that point, Mary and I gasped. "That long?" we both exclaimed in disbelief, as if Jerry Jean broke the world record for longest kiss ever.

The interrogation didn't stop there. "Did he put his arm around you?" Mary continued, her eyes wide with curiosity. But Jerry Jean drew the line—clamming up, refusing to give away any more secrets.

Thinking back now, I laugh how Wonder Bread perfectly encapsulated Jerry Jean's innocent belief in anything advertised on TV. The slogan claimed, "Wonder Bread builds strong bodies twelve ways," and she believed it with such conviction that it was almost impossible to challenge her. I once asked her why she only ate Wonder Bread. Without missing a beat, she responded with absolute certainty, "Because Wonder Bread builds strong bodies twelve ways."

I was intrigued with how easily we accept things when they're packaged nicely and repeated enough times. It was amusing, yet it sparked something deeper in me, a realization that maybe we shouldn't take everything at face value. Jerry Jean, bless her heart, believed it all—if it was on TV, it had to be true. We loved her for it, but it made me wonder what else we blindly accepted.

• • •

It seemed like life was finally on Easy Street, like the path ahead smoothed out with all those bumps leveled off. But life has a way of shaking things up in the most unexpected ways.

One afternoon, while my mother was going about her usual chore of sorting the laundry, something caught her attention. She stopped abruptly, as though she saw a ghost. Holding up one of Wayne's shirts, her eyes locked onto the collar. There it was—clear as day—a smudge of pink lipstick.

She froze, staring at the small mark. Then, with rising fury, she shrieked, "I hate pink lipstick! This isn't mine—I only wear peach!" Her voice was sharp and trembling, a mixture of disbelief and devastation. She clutched the stained shirt like it held the answer to all her heartbroken questions. Her mind raced with possibilities. What did this mean? How could this happen? The shock turned into a full storm of emotions.

By the time Wayne walked through the door, expecting dinner as usual, he was met with something entirely different—hell to pay, as they say. The house erupted into chaos, filled with crying, shouting, and adamant denials. The air crackled with tension, and suddenly, the steady rhythm of our lives felt disrupted, as if nothing was as certain as it once seemed.

FROM MOB TIES TO MIRACLES

CHAPTER 6

LOCKED OUT: THE DREAM OF COLLEGE THAT WASN'T

EVEN AMID THE STORM OF DOMESTIC TENSIONS, LIFE PRESSED on. My parents remained focused, continuing their steady rise up the socioeconomic ladder, as if their efforts could negate Wayne's unfaithfulness. After selling the house on Bangert for twice what my mother paid for it, they moved to a more rural area called Arnold, and when the time was right, sold that home as well, doubling their equity once again. By the summer of 1971, my mother had her sights on a larger home with more room—because for her, there was always a bigger vision, a grander goal just within reach.

You could never accuse my mother of being lazy or a kept woman—far from it. She was the driving force behind my stepfather, always urging him to aim higher. Tirelessly working alongside him, my mother possessed determination that was evident in every aspect of their growing success. While Wayne expanded the business, branching into non-food products like toiletries, linens, school supplies, and food containers, my mother supported his every move. His efforts paid off, securing contracts with well-known brands and placing his merchandise in every privately owned supermarket across the greater St. Louis area.

Despite the occasionally thunderous bumps, life had its remarkable moments. It was clear my parents were on a winning streak, and nothing—not even a pink lipstick smudge—could deter their shared ambition. It seemed nothing—neither domestic discord nor unforeseen setbacks—could derail their shared ambition to climb higher. Their momentum carried them forward, unshaken, toward greater success.

My mother scouted neighborhoods in southwest St. Louis. Astute and determined, she was the most driven person I've ever known—and I've met many successful people. One day, she drove through Lakeshire, a private, upscale neighborhood. The houses were possibly beyond their means, but she loved what she saw. She visited an open house—a colonial-style, white-brick home with four bedrooms and two baths—and fell in love instantly, promising to return with Wayne.

10002 Lakeside Drive represented prestige: a corner lot in a beautiful neighborhood of sprawling properties, with nearly a half-acre to claim as our own. The place was secluded, with perfectly manicured lawns and towering trees that whispered of old money separating the stately homes. But beneath the allure, there was tension—a gamble on my parents' part. Could we truly fit in here? Could we afford it long-term? What were the schools like? And how would our family of six adjust to this new chapter?

Wayne only needed one look. He was sold. He knew the numbers inside and out—solid income, reliable tax returns, and a fierce drive to be the perfect provider. This wasn't just a house; it was a gleaming symbol of their climb, a badge of their rising success.

Once again, my parents were on the path to glory.

Lakeside was more than just a charming home; it was a shared dream, a canvas that invited each of us to leave our personal touch upon it. There was an enchantment there, a divine sense that a house could truly unite our family in this new chapter. We were brimming with ideas—each one eager to make this place our own.

My mother, with her newfound flair for design, led the way. She took interior design classes and joined the Lakeshire Garden Club, mingling with the lovely and gracious ladies of the neighborhood. There, in our new home, her creativity truly blossomed. Every room became her masterpiece, pushing away from past utilitarian choices into a refined elegance and artistic sophistication. Each square foot bore the mark of Mom's vision, turning our house into something extraordinary, a reflection of her growth and a space that embraced us all.

My parents' love evolved over the years, seasoned like a deep friendship that comes with time and shared experiences. It wasn't the fiery passion of new love, but something more enduring took its place, something built on mutual respect and companionship. Together, they were unstoppable—a powerhouse duo whose strength came from their unwavering support of each other.

My mother truly loved Wayne, and Wayne couldn't imagine living with anyone else. Yet, in the midst of living their dreams, they each became so absorbed in their own pursuits that they unintentionally took each other for granted.

Even so, they remained each other's foundation, always pushing toward greater success. Their bond, though less about grand gestures and more about a shared sense of purpose, was unbreakable. They may have been busy with their commitments to home and family, but beneath it was a deeply rooted partnership that knew no limits. Together, they kept climbing, secure in the knowledge that whatever challenges came their way, they would face them side by side.

Within a month of moving into our Lakeshire home, twenty-eight-year-old Wayne, who fully embraced his role as a successful businessman, husband, and father of four, decided to expand the business. He purchased a refrigerated truck to start selling cold products. I remember he measured the garage, worried the neighbors might complain if he parked the truck in the driveway. Then he found a solution—a large space behind the house where the truck could be tucked out of sight.

Wayne perfected his recipe for success, carefully crafting an image that belied his true achievements. By day, he drove an old, worn truck, his baggy trousers and rugged Oxfords reflecting a deliberate modesty. This carefully maintained appearance, designed to suggest financial struggle, was part of a calculated facade intended to win favor and trust. In contrast, my mother's sleek Cadillac sat polished and waiting in the garage, a stark reminder of the wealth Wayne chose not to flaunt. To the outside world, he appeared to be scraping by. Reflecting now, I wonder if that understated appearance was not only a deliberate choice but also an authentic reflection of Wayne's true nature.

But the toll of years of hard work was starting to show. Wayne developed a slight limp, and his hairline receded, giving him a more weathered look. At just five-foot-seven, his self-consciousness about his height was exacerbated by these physical changes. Despite these signs of aging, his spirit remained undiminished. He carried himself with the same quiet confidence and unshakable resolve that always defined him.

Beneath his charming exterior, Wayne was deeply introspective, carefully concealing much of his true self. We had frequent conversations about dieting—we were always mindful of our weight. Yet, when my mother glanced disapprovingly at the belly Wayne was beginning to grow, Wayne would assert with a certain conviction, "I need this extra weight for when I get cancer and need the reserves." His words seemed odd at the time, but knowing both his parents had died of cancer, I dismissed them, sensing a deeper, almost providential undertone in his remarks.

• • •

Every morning, Wayne was my alarm clock. "Karen," he called up to me from the foot of the stairs, "it's time to get up." That was my cue to rouse my sisters and get us all ready for school and church on Sundays. He often snuck out early on Sundays to grab donuts before anyone else was awake. We'd come downstairs to a box of treats specially chosen for each of us, with my beloved Boston creme always waiting.

Disagreements in a house of five females were inevitable, but Wayne was the consummate diplomat. "We need to talk, girls," he'd say. And we'd talk—sometimes until we were begging to stop talking and get back to our day. Wayne was a peacekeeper, never afraid to apologize if he thought it was warranted. He was a man of deep humility and boundless care.

It's easy to overlook, but Wayne was a divine blessing, an answer to our prayers. His presence, from his arrival to his departure, was nothing short of providential, a testament to the perfect timing and grace that guided us.

I was approaching my last year of high school when my mother started pushing me to take secretarial classes. I loved math and science, but I decided to appease Mom. She argued that I could always fall back on secretarial skills, no matter what career path I chose.

In my senior year, my student counselor and I started exploring universities and career options. The University of Kansas had an amazing theater program, and I was thrilled at the thought of applying. The idea of diving into something that genuinely excited me filled me with a sense of hope and anticipation.

One night, I brought up the topic of finances with my mother. I wanted to know if I would qualify for financial aid to help cover tuition. Without skipping a beat, Mom looked at me and said, "We can't afford it. I didn't go to college, and you'll make a great secretary. Just imagine all the nice men you'll meet! I wish I could've done that."

I was stunned speechless. Her words struck me like a bolt of lightning, and I felt as though the ground had been ripped out from under me. Silent, I turned away, the weight of her words crashing into me like an avalanche, and retreated to my room, moving like I was walking through a thick, suffocating fog. Every step felt heavier, each one further from the world I once knew. The door clicked shut behind me, and I collapsed onto my bed, burying my face in the pillow, desperate to drown out the reality of what my mother just said. I cried, but it wasn't just sadness—it was like my very future was unraveling before me. I wanted to flee from everything, to escape from a life that no longer offered any hope. Exhaustion eventually took over, and I fell into a sleep that felt as empty and distant as the future I once imagined for myself.

It felt as if my future had been yanked away in an instant. All my friends were heading to college, and here I was, expected to settle for becoming a secretary—and what, marry my boss?

That moment set into motion a spiral of doubt and confusion. That missed opportunity, something I once assumed was essential to discovering who I was and the knowledge needed to navigate my talents and desires, left me stifled, unable to fully explore or even begin to define my identity. Without that stepping stone, I found myself desperately seeking Karen, living aimlessly and grasping at anything to fill the void, but I felt like a failure. For the next few years, I couldn't escape that feeling, even as I tried to convince myself that I'd find another way.

At first, I denied it—telling myself it would get better, that somehow I'd find another way. Then anger set in, simmering beneath the surface as I questioned why my dreams were so easily discarded. I bargained with myself, with life, clinging to the hope that things could still change, that I might carve out a different path. But when nothing shifted, depression wrapped around me like a heavy fog. I carried that weight with me everywhere, moving through daily life in slow motion, disconnected from the future I once envisioned. Eventually, there came a reluctant acceptance—not because I was at peace with my fate, but because I had no choice. I was living it.

It took three long years to begin to recover, and though I moved forward, the loss of those dreams lingered.

• • •

After my high school graduation, my mother selfishly was content to have my company for the summer. By the fall of 1974, she advanced her goals for my life, outfitting me in what she considered the perfect ensemble for job interviews. From my perspective, every inch of fabric was awful: a navy polyester dress paired with my Coke-bottle glasses and white gloves. I wore it to my first interview at a small insurance company. To my surprise, I was hired.

The managing director may have felt sorry for me when he hired me, but he couldn't ignore my skills. I was a master at shorthand and typing, able to perform the most demanding tasks. He was genuinely impressed by my professionalism and efficiency.

Still, I hated every moment of the job. It was demeaning, as I was capable of so much more. I tried other jobs, but none fulfilled me.

My mother, who was once my guide and protector, morphed into a relentless tyrant. I still lived with her, and what began as simple household expectations escalated into outright demands. She took a significant portion of my salary for rent and food, pushing the boundaries of our relationship. We became adversaries, clashing over the smallest things. On her bad days—especially when her moods were fierce—it felt like she was no longer the mother I once knew but someone else, someone darker. She was hateful and aggressive, almost acting as one who was demon-possessed. Each argument fueled my desperation to escape, to find my own apartment and reclaim my freedom.

Fortunately, I landed a job as a nurse's assistant at Shriners Hospital for Crippled Children, a prestigious institution nestled in the affluent suburb of Ladue. In my quest for independence and self-discovery, I frequented the Frontenac Mall after work, where I fell in love with Saks Fifth Avenue. Though I wore a uniform during the day, I began investing in attractive new clothes and finally ditched my thick, Coke-bottle glasses for contact lenses.

After a few months, the hospital administrator, aware of the turmoil at home, offered me a room in the dormitory residence next to the hospital. I was ecstatic—finally, I had peace of mind and a stable job in a respected environment.

Taking care of the children at the hospital was more than a job—it was a profoundly moving and transformative experience. These were fragile, vulnerable children, many from broken homes, who lived with physical handicaps that required intense care. Their needs far overshadowed my own, pulling me into their world of suffering, hope, and resilience. Every morning as I walked down the hall, the soft, excited whispers spread through the ward like a gentle wave: "Nurse Karen is here! Nurse Karen is here!" Their small, expectant faces would light up the room, looking to me for care and the tenderness and attention their young hearts craved.

The warmth of their joy was infectious, creating a kind of magic that warmed even the coldest mornings. If I could have, I would have taken every one of them home. I grew to love them as if they were my own. But that love also brought the heartbreak of witnessing their harrowing struggles—children enduring burns, heart conditions, physical abuse, amputations, craniofacial deformities, orthopedic challenges, and spinal cord injuries. These children weren't just in need of medical treatment; they desperately needed the human touch, love, and reassurance that someone was there for them.

Unfortunately, many of my colleagues, perhaps as a product of the job's emotional toll, were callous and robotic in their care. This detached approach only deepened the children's fear and vulnerability, hindering their recuperation. But as "Nurse Karen," I was their mom, angel, sweetheart, and protector. My heart was wide open to them, and I cherished that sacred bond, knowing that in their most fragile moments, I was their safe harbor.

After intense days with the children at the hospital, I returned to my apartment completely spent, emotionally drained and longing for someone to talk to. The work took everything out of me—physically, mentally, and emotionally. Instead of finding solace, I felt aimless, drifting through life without direction. On weekends, I sought escape in popular dance clubs, losing myself in the latest dance moves and staying until the lights dimmed, signaling the end of another empty night. I met countless men, but none stirred any real desire in me. I often went to a club called Jericho's, spending entire weekends mingling and dancing with strangers, letting the music and vibrant energy transport me into a glamorous illusion. For those fleeting hours, I felt like someone else, swept away by the night. But when the music stopped and the lights came back on, reality returned, leaving me in my quiet apartment, falling asleep from sheer exhaustion, the weight of life pressing down on me.

The pressure of my job, combined with the lack of support from family and friends, pushed me into a dangerous spiral. As a perfectionist, I became obsessed with controlling my weight, convincing myself that trimming down was the answer to everything wrong in my life. But my determination quickly turned into something more destructive, and I started starving myself. Eventually, anorexia took control, leaving me dangerously weak. One Saturday morning, I lay on my apartment floor, so frail I could barely move. With my last bit of strength, I called my mother. She arrived with my sister Mary, and they rushed me to the emergency room. I was admitted with extreme malnutrition, dehydration, and a failing liver.

I spent a week in the hospital being nursed back to health. My struggle with anorexia had come perilously close to ending my life, but that harrowing experience ignited a profound resolve within me. I vowed never to let it control me again. In that vulnerable state, I prayed to God, pleading for life and promising that if He granted me a second chance, I would commit myself to seeking a relationship with Him.

Upon my return to work, I was called in by the administrator, who expressed concern for my well-being and inquired about my recent absence. Then she delivered heartbreaking news: one of the little girls on the ward had passed away. The gravity of this revelation was crushing, and I grappled with whether I had the fortitude to carry on.

My sense of regret and understanding was profound. Resigning under such emotionally charged circumstances was an excruciating decision, but I had to prioritize my own well-being. My time at Shriners had profoundly affected me, not only due to the deep affection I had for the children but also because of the emotional toll the work exacted on my spirit.

• • •

Moving back in with my family offered a chance for some much-needed rest and reconciliation. Despite the tension that often marked my relationship with my mother, she was eager to help me get back on my feet. I knew she loved deeply, but love didn't always come easily to her. She grew up in a highly dysfunctional family, fighting to survive. Could I really blame her for the way she was? I'm not sure she ever fully grasped her own dysfunction or knew how to create a new path forward. But for a short while, at least, it was good to be home. It was a quiet reprieve, a pause to reflect, but I couldn't stay there forever.

The yearning for something more pulled at me, and at twenty-one, seeking a new experience with a more mature outlook, I stepped into a club at Westport Plaza. The moment I entered, I was enveloped in an atmosphere of sophisticated elegance. The venue was adorned with soft, dazzling lights that cascaded over sleek surfaces and the dance floor, creating a chic and mesmerizing ambiance—so different from the familiar, yet stifling, world I had just left behind.

The sound system was nothing short of extraordinary, delivering the pulsating beats of 1975 classics—"Rock the Boat," "Philadelphia Freedom," "Jive Talkin'," and "The Hustle"—with crystal clarity. The air was charged with the rhythmic groove of disco, and the latest dance craze, The Bump, had everyone on their feet. The music's vibrant energy mingled effortlessly with the elegantly dressed crowd, each note resonating through the room and adding to the club's exhilarating charm.

At the bar, an attractive man of Asian descent captured my attention. Not much taller than my five-foot, two-inch frame, he had jet-black hair that framed a face exuding charm and cheer. His affable demeanor was magnetic, and his body language—an intriguing blend of self-control and boldness—drew me in.

My successful modus operandi was still in play, my go-to approach that never failed. Maybe it was my youthful naivety, my non-threatening and friendly demeanor, that made it easy for me to turn strangers into friends. Within five minutes, we formally introduced ourselves, as the music and ambiance of the club began to lift my spirits, adding a spark of energy to the evening. He introduced himself as Michael Adachi. He and his colleagues were from Gardner Advertising, and he managed the Anheuser-Busch account. Knowing that only added to the excitement of the evening.

ACT 2

MAKING MY WAY

CHAPTER 7

CUSHIONS, CALAMITY, AND CALIFORNIA DREAMIN': MY LIFE IN SITCOM STYLE

GIVEN MY FATHER'S INFAMOUS RELATIONSHIP WITH THE Anheuser-Busch Credit Union, it almost felt like a cosmic joke when Michael casually mentioned he managed the Anheuser-Busch account. Clearly, bringing up my father's "shadowed" history with Anheuser-Busch was not the best icebreaker for this conversation. It was as if the universe was giving me a little wink, reminding me that some connections are better left unsaid.

Michael, with his high social intellect and infectious energy, was impossible not to like. His spirited nature and ability to make everyone laugh was magnetic. He offered me a drink, which I accepted, and I was immediately captivated by his world.

I knew nothing about advertising, but I wanted to learn everything—from his work at Gardner Advertising to his Japanese heritage and what it meant to manage the Anheuser-Busch account. As the night wore on, his genuine interest in me became more apparent, and before long, he invited me to dinner.

Over dinner, Michael shared more about his background. He was a third-generation Japanese American, or Sansei, as he explained, offering a bit of conversation in Japanese, a language he learned from his parents while growing up in Cincinnati, Ohio. Michael lit up when discussing his heritage. He was different from other men I met—polite, formal, and always a gentleman. His modest, mild, and docile nature, paired with an unwavering sense of propriety, drew me in even further.

Given my complicated relationship with my father, I was naturally wary of men who led with aggression. But Michael won my heart in no time. I approached him cautiously at first, but I was drawn to his quick wit, intelligence, ambition, and energy. We had so much fun together, and within a few months, we decided to get married and start a life together.

Michael, at thirty-one years old and ten years my senior, was ready to settle down. For him, our marriage was more than love—it was a calculated step forward in his career. Unlike the glamour of the *Mad Men* era, where bold pitches and whiskey-fueled lunches defined success, Michael saw his five-foot-four frame and Japanese American heritage as factors requiring a different kind of strategy. He believed that marrying a young, midwestern blonde like me not only enhanced his desired image but also projected the kind of stability and status that could quietly bolster his credibility in an industry still deeply influenced by appearances.

With me by his side, Michael boldly pursued new opportunities, landing a promising sales position with D'Arcy-MacManus and Masius Advertising in the heart of downtown Chicago. Eager to embrace our destiny and chart our career paths, we moved to Chicago after a small wedding with friends and family.

From my perspective, Michael was my savior and protector, and his delight in my fascination was quite evident. He was eager to show me off and was deeply in love with his new bride.

Our marriage blossomed like a timeless melody—vibrant and infectious. It began with a mix of youthful playfulness and a yearning for the sophistication we would grow into, layering trust, laughter, and ambition like a cherished song that deepens with every chord, each progression bringing new depth and meaning, like the leap from a simple chord to the richness of a seventh interval.

Our shared joy was light and spontaneous, turning even simple moments into something extraordinary. We moved through life together, driven by a soulful rhythm that kept us in sync and propelled us forward. Every challenge we faced was met with boldness and unity.

Though Michael's dance moves were a bit on the awkward side—his "Do the Dog" routine was so cringeworthy, I pretended I wasn't with him—our marriage was a dance of its own kind. It was dynamic and quickly evolving, propelled with a momentum that kept us moving and growing, even if his rhythm was questionable. What we had was uniquely ours—a mix of enthusiasm, youthful naivete, and the kind of humor that made even the most embarrassing moments positively unforgettable.

The solid grounding of Michael and my unpredictable nature were always destined to clash, like two freight trains barreling down different tracks. Michael was the embodiment of stability—grounded, deliberate, and methodical. He built his life with careful planning, a steady trajectory aligned with his ambitions. I, on the other hand, thrived in spontaneity—impulsive, fiery, and unrestrained in my pursuit of experience. While he envisioned the long game, I leapt headfirst into the chaos of the present.

For Michael, I must have appeared as the spark to ignite his structured existence; to me, he was the anchor I didn't know I needed. Together, we formed a volatile concoction of strategy and spontaneity—his thoughtful planning set against my unfiltered energy. Our differences often collided in unexpected ways, creating a tension both exhilarating and difficult, as if our paths were constantly crossing, each of us trying to steer our different tracks into alignment.

We were two small people with big dreams, ready to soar to new heights, inseparable and deeply in love, united by our unwavering belief in the power of love to make the impossible seem possible.

We were floating on cloud nine, and the company footed the bill for our move. Bekins Moving and Storage rolled up to whisk away our wildly eclectic collection: a mid-century orange sofa, two more orange butterfly chairs (because clearly, we were committed to a life in citrus hues—at least we had a theme: "rustic meets orange"), a full-sized bed that had survived Michael's childhood, battered nightstands that had seen better days, a large oak wine barrel served as our dining table, a wooden crate doubling as a coffee table, and a media cabinet that proudly housed an ancient TV and radio combo. With wardrobe boxes packed to the gills, we took off, riding a wave of youthful naivete and dizzying confidence, utterly convinced the big city wasn't just ready for our grand ambitions but was eagerly awaiting our arrival and would roll out the red carpet for us.

We found a one-bedroom apartment perched on the thirty-first floor of Burton Way, just off Lake Shore Drive. The cityscape unfolded before us, a dazzling tapestry of lights and movement that seemed to extend endlessly. Our apartment featured a valet and easy access to the vibrant Near North neighborhood, and we were mere steps from Lake Michigan and the bustling heart of Michigan Avenue.

Sirens and traffic sounds rose through the night, adding to the city's symphony—a stark yet thrilling contrast to the tranquil suburbs we had left behind. This new city life felt like a grand adventure, where every sound and sight played a part of our exciting new chapter.

Michael and I were eager to dive into our new lives, each of us forging our own paths toward success. His daily commute was a breeze, with his office just a stone's throw away. This allowed him to immerse himself in his burgeoning career. Meanwhile, I meticulously charted my own course through Chicago's vast landscape of opportunities, from advertising agencies to video production firms and talent agencies.

In the mid-'70s, Chicago exuded glamour and pizzazz. Its skyline glittered like a disco ball, blending modern high-rises with timeless, classic architecture. Below, the streets hummed with vibrant energy, as if the city were dancing to its own rhythm.

By night, Chicago turned into a spectacle of elegance and excitement. There were swanky jazz clubs where everyone pretended to be refined connoisseurs and disco hotspots where flared pants and boogie moves reigned supreme. A blast of sophisticated revelers sported outfits that were so sleek you wondered if they were participating in a fashion contest.

With a clear focus on my aspirations to be an actress and character model, I dove headfirst into the glamorous world of Chicago's modeling scene. The petite models in demand at McCormick Place indicated I had a real shot to make a name for myself. I eagerly took on roles representing manufacturers at high-profile events like the Sporting Goods Convention, Auto Shows, and Housewares Show, reveling in every chance to showcase the latest and greatest state-of-the-art products.

The excitement continued to build as I encountered an array of celebrities. Meeting icons such as Chicago Bears quarterback Bob Avellini and the entire Chicago Cubs roster became par for course while on the job. Jack Sander, chairman of the Chicago Mercantile Exchange, was a towering figure in Chicago's financial world, renowned for his influence in shaping the city's futures trading landscape. His name carried weight in business and society alike, symbolizing both financial acumen and elite connections. His presence added another layer of prestige to the experience—a world where ambition and opportunity intertwined with a touch of celebrity sparkle, making each moment uniquely unforgettable.

Joining a talent agency proved to be a pivotal move, leading to various gigs, including television commercials for the American Chiropractics, which earned accolades in the medical industry, as well as a ski clothing manufacturer, and Montgomery Ward. The steady stream of work with exclusive agencies hinted at a promising future.

As my career gained momentum, Michael was climbing the corporate ladder, his professional achievements a testament to his dedication and talent. Our careers were blossoming in tandem, each success adding fuel to our shared ambitions as we ventured into this thrilling new chapter together.

Reflecting on those years, I can't help but feel a deep sense of gratitude for the richly vibrant experiences that adorned our lives. Our two years in Chicago mirrored the city—dazzling, dynamic, and full of life.

On weekends, we celebrated our professional triumphs and personal milestones, immersing ourselves in the city's splendor. Often, we retreated to the intimate charm of live piano bars, which served as the perfect soundtrack to our evenings. They created an atmosphere of sophistication and warmth, turning each celebration into something even more enchanting.

During this time, I landed a part-time gig at Saks Fifth Avenue and treated myself to a professional business suit—after all, nothing says "I've arrived" like a chic pantsuit. However, my first foray into the world of tailored fashion was a classic case of "measure twice, cut once" gone hilariously awry. I measured myself like a pro—or so I thought. Somehow, the pants accompanying the suit were designed for a giant. What was supposed to be a sleek, sophisticated look featured pants that were now humorously short, leaving me with a gorgeous beige jacket and no usable pants! Despite my best efforts, there was no saving the pants. No amount of tugging, pleading, or creative sewing could stretch them to the appropriate length.

Around that time, Boz Scaggs's "Lowdown" was all the rage, and it became the soundtrack to our lives in Chicago. The song's smooth, funky rhythm and sultry grooves perfectly captured the city's high-energy nightlife, as if it were written for that moment in our lives. With its seductive bass lines, jazzy undertones, and Scaggs' effortlessly cool vocals, "Lowdown" embodied the stylish savoir faire of Chicago's club scene. The track's blend of soul and funk evoked a sense of effortless chic, much like the fusion of opulence and vibrancy that surrounded us at every turn.

After a beautiful meal, Michael and I would step into a dimly lit lounge, where the air was thick with expensive perfume and cigar smoke. The soft hum of conversation and the clinking of glasses filled the room, creating an intimate backdrop.

On the dance floor, we swayed to deep rhythms as the music drifted through the open windows onto the sidewalks of Rush Street. It was a time when being in love with life—and with Michael—felt like the most natural thing in the world.

• • •

On Sundays, Michael and I would settle in to watch our favorite concerts on television as Arthur Fiedler conducted the Boston Pops.

We were both captivated by the enchanting music and vowed we would go to New England at some point. We had a close-knit group of friends—Michael's colleagues who lived in our building, and we decided to host them for a homemade chili night, the perfect choice for crisp fall evenings. Eagerly anticipating the event, I faced a pressing need for a new sofa. Instead, I removed the loose cushion covers and washed them.

Saturday night arrived with a cocktail of excitement and dread. The cushion covers, now shrunken to half their original size, turned our once-modest sofa into a circus act, with cushions puffed up like mini umbrellas ready to take flight. But I was determined to save the evening with a feast that would impress—so out came the dehydrated Hungry Jack mashed potatoes and steaks for the grill. We were all set to dazzle our "established" young friends—or so we foolishly believed.

The night quickly spiraled into the kind of memorable disaster made for sitcoms. Our guests tried to keep their straight faces as they perched on the absurdly distorted sofa. But the real kicker came when Bob, our lovable, husky friend with a voice like a grizzly bear, growled out, "Oh, Hungry Jack! I love Hungry Jacks!" My face turned every shade of red. As for that box of Hungry Jack, it found a permanent home in the trash can—without any tears shed.

• • •

After a year in the city, we felt a change of scenery might be beneficial, so we relocated to Evanston, just steps from the Northwestern University campus. The town offered sandy beaches, historic mansions on landscaped boulevards, beautiful parks with one of the largest and most diverse arts and theater communities, but the harsh winters, with their relentless lake-effect snow, were a stark contrast to the milder climates of Cincinnati and St. Louis. As the snow accumulated, our thoughts increasingly turned to sunnier locales—especially Los Angeles, where Michael's sister and her family lived. The allure of the West Coast grew ever stronger.

As our thoughts increasingly turned toward sunnier locales, a promising opportunity arose. Michael secured an interview with a Pepsi-owned radio station in Bel Air, California. We strategized how he might leverage the growing emphasis on diversity in corporate HR platforms. While Michael's Japanese heritage was an asset, he possessed everything the station executives were looking for: midwestern charm, strong work ethic, warm personality, impressive credentials, and, of course, the added bonus of a lovely wife by his side.

Michael landed the job, and our move to an upscale one-bedroom apartment in Beverly Hills felt like a dream come true. We were thrilled to be in the coveted 90210 zip code, convinced we had arrived. Michael's daily commute was an adventure on its own, as he navigated the narrow, winding roads up to KJOI Radio, which was perched nearly 1,000 feet above Los Angeles. The scenic drive through the city's most affluent neighborhoods, past grand mansions and lush landscapes, became a weekend ritual. As a result of the steep drive, we replaced brake pads almost as frequently as we changed weekend plans.

Our fascination with the comedy series *WKRP in Cincinnati* deepened our sense of surrealism, as the show's humorous take on the radio business seemed to mirror our lives with uncanny accuracy. Michael, hailing from Cincinnati, often found his reflection in the characters, perhaps envisioning me as Loni Anderson in our own real-life sitcom. This parallel made the industry feel like a perfect fit for him, and together, we eagerly embraced this thrilling new chapter, stepping into roles that felt both familiar and exhilarating.

Now that we were in California, Michael seized the opportunity to play golf nearly every day, and the sport quickly became his favorite pastime. Sundays were particularly amusing. He would promise to attend Catholic services as I headed to my Presbyterian church, only to slip his golf clubs into the trunk.

Despite Michael's assurances, I had my doubts about his church attendance. His proof came in the form of a church program, which he presented to me each week. I suspect he spent the morning on the golf course and snatched the program to maintain his alibi. Michael was determined to become the best golfer in Los Angeles, and who could blame him? The golf clubs in West LA were irresistible.

As Michael continued to immerse himself in the advertising business, I embarked on a new professional adventure. I landed a position at I. Magnin, where I worked with high-end couture women's clothing. There, I sold designer outfits to celebrities such as Cher and Neil Diamond, as well as a host of B-list actresses. Our store hosted fashion shows featuring renowned designers like Givenchy, Chanel, Donna Karan, and Yves Saint Laurent. The world of high fashion added sparkle to our California experience, seamlessly blending with the allure of our new life.

Living in Beverly Hills with Michael working in Bel Air, our lives were intertwined with the city's elite. This proximity afforded us a wealth of exclusive opportunities. We frequently received tickets to film screenings before movies hit theaters and enjoyed dining in upscale restaurants, thanks to our "script"—advertising money provided by clients on the radio. These scripts, typically in increments of $10 and $20 and sometimes $100 allowed us to savor the finer things in life while mingling with Hollywood's glitterati.

Our Beverly Hills lifestyle, complemented by these perks, made every day a step into a glamorous, star-studded world.

• • •

When Michael had to work late, Betty Kraus and I ventured out together. Fifty years older than me, Betty was a treasure trove of life lessons. She lived a few blocks from the store on Wilshire Boulevard and continued working with the enthusiasm of someone half her age. Together, we hit the town, using my "script" to live as the high-society ladies of Beverly Hills—a seeming mother-daughter duo with a flair for extravagance.

One evening at a posh restaurant, we had a hundred dollars of leftover script that couldn't be saved for another day. Betty, ever resourceful and practical, stuffed her enormous handbag with sugar and salt packets and insisted we spend the remaining funds on desserts. She then ordered every dessert on the menu, which arrived at our table in two giant boxes. The sight must have been something to behold—a veritable dessert parade to go. We left an impression, if not on our fellow diners and the restaurant's dessert cart.

Betty and I had a work relationship that felt like we were in a spy thriller. Our mission: Identify the big spenders rather than thwart international conspiracies. Betty, with her keen eyes and stealthy tactics, could spot a high roller from a mile away. Watching her in action was like witnessing a seasoned general preparing for battle, except our battleground was the high-end fashion floor of I. Magnin.

On top of expert client-spotting skills, Betty deployed the superb sales strategy. "Just take it home," I heard her say a million times. "If you don't like it, bring it back." It was pure genius, and it worked like magic, convincing customers to take the plunge with no long-term obligation required. Of course, no one ever returned any purchases. After all, who wants to go through the hassle of returning fabulous clothes? It's easier to keep them.

Each day, I couldn't wait to get to work and absorb the esprit of Betty Kraus, the cherished maître of sales. With her élégance and perspicacité, she effortlessly drew customers in, and her approach— "Just take it home; if you don't like it, bring it back"—was pure audacity.

Learning from Betty was a master class, and I was eager to develop my own style in the Betty Kraus tradition. No one else could come close to her mastery. It was no wonder Betty won numerous store awards for most sales—her bold approach made her untouchable. I loved Betty Kraus and her unforgettable techniques.

• • •

Michael's sister, Kally, and Grandma Sugimoto lived in Los Angeles. Knowing they would eventually come over for dinner, we decided to upgrade our furniture. We envisioned a refined décor that would blend beautifully with blues and beiges, accented by Japanese influences. Our pièce de résistance was a tufted floral sofa with matching chairs—dignified yet inviting.

Art was a must, but ever-frugal Michael kept us on a tight budget. Not to be deterred, I channeled my inner artist, painting serene Japanese-style countryside watercolors and a graceful lady in a kimono. We had them professionally framed, adding a personal but cultured touch to our home. In the meantime, Michael struck gold at a garage sale, discovering a stunning antique silk fan adorned with cranes in a tranquil lakeside landscape. He beamed over his find that cost just a few dollars. We framed the fan, which spanned the full length of our TV console, in custom plexiglass, a perfect focal point tying everything together with the right amount of panache. The room came together quite nicely, a harmonious blend of provincial style and our unique personal flair.

Our apartment was perfectly situated, backing up to the famous restaurant row on La Cienega. On warm summer evenings, the tantalizing aromas of Lawry's Steak House wafted through the air, mingling with the scent of jasmine, bird-of-paradise flowers and swaying palm trees outside our window. Beyond our living room, a lovely swimming pool shimmered, adding to the idyllic setting.

Michael took pride in managing our finances down to the last penny. Every night, he took ten dollars from our cash reserves and placed it neatly in my nightstand. That modest sum covered my bus fare to and from work, plus lunch money—no more, no less. He favored being my protector and taught me how to manage a checkbook, how to budget and plan for the future, the importance of taking a job seriously, and, above all, that my word was my bond.

Michael quickly became beloved in Beverly Hills, and before long, we were browsing potential homes in the neighborhood. Of course, given the societal norms of the time, I couldn't be listed on the mortgage application—women were considered a risky addition to such paperwork. The reasoning was rooted in outdated beliefs that a woman might get pregnant and be unable to work, making her an unpredictable financial liability. Despite this, we were excited about our future, dreaming of putting down roots in this iconic city.

Amid our life in Beverly Hills, I became intrigued with dabbling in film work. Dreams of the silver screen filled my mind, driving me to try my hand as an extra during my vacations and off days. It wasn't long before an opportunity came my way. *Sergeant Pepper's Lonely Hearts Club Band* was being filmed, and I was thrilled to be chosen as an extra. The experience was nothing short of exhilarating, working on such a vibrant and fun set with none other than Robert Burns and the Bee Gees. It was a taste of the Hollywood magic I desired, adding another layer of excitement to our Beverly Hills adventure.

The first day on set, the director approached me with an unexpected assignment. He directed me toward Andy Gibb—yes, *the* Andy Gibb—and told me I'd be playing an aggressive fan. My role? To grab Andy and give him a great big kiss.

I was taken aback. This wasn't just a background role; it was something more, something that challenged my comfort level and commitment to my husband. Suddenly, the glamour of Hollywood tarnished. It was a moment straight out of "A Chorus Line: Nothing," in which the dream you've chased feels off-key, the shine dulled by reality. I hesitated and then bowed out, politely saying no. The director's stern, surprised look said it all—"You're done," and I was.

They didn't invite me back, and just like that, my Hollywood dream fizzled before it began. Still, I was in the movie, and that day wasn't a total loss. I danced to the music and met some incredible actors. But the experience left me with a bittersweet taste—I realized that sometimes, chasing dreams doesn't go as planned.

Later, I left I. Magnum for a sales position at Celine of Paris on Rodeo Drive. The allure of working on one of the most famous streets in the world, surrounded by celebrities, was enticing. Maurice Gibb once walked into the store and asked me to join him and his brother, Andy Gibb, for a day on the town. He was persistent, practically begging, unwilling to notice my wedding ring. Once again, I was at a crossroads. Realizing the potential for trouble, I bowed out a second time.

• • •

Despite the glamour and the brushes with fame, a nagging feeling of disillusionment began to settle in. I couldn't shake the sense that this business, with all its glitz and glitter, was hollow at its core. It was a world where hard work often went unnoticed, only a lucky few reaped rewards, and many "has-beens"—older, mature actors—clung to a fading dream, wasting their lives away in pursuit of something that might never come.

That moment, I made a decision. There was no path forward in a business that didn't value perseverance or reward dedication over time. My disillusionment was too deep, and I resolved to step away, knowing the Hollywood dream wasn't for me.

With Hollywood's bright lights losing its luster, I was drawn back to the fashion world, a realm where creativity met practicality. Michael, ever pragmatic, encouraged me to pursue something more substantial. Together, we explored college grants and opportunities to further my education. However, Michael was adamant—he wouldn't fund my college career outright. His plan was for me to continue working full-time while attending school in the evenings.

Luckily, UCLA offered a program tailored for people like me—those eager to dive deep into the fashion industry. They taught everything from fabric acquisition in Asia to mastering the ins and outs of manufacturing, wholesaling, and retail. It was an opportunity to learn every facet of the business. Despite the challenges, I was determined to seize it.

I enrolled in the program and quickly absorbed everything it had to offer. Combining my exclusive retail background with my new studies at UCLA, I crafted an impressive resume and landed what seemed the perfect job in the heart of the Los Angeles Garment District at the Apparel Mart. This position was the epitome of hands-on learning, a defining experience.

I immersed myself completely in every facet of the garment industry, learning the ins and outs of the entire business. From design and production to marketing and retail, I gained a thorough understanding of how each part connected and contributed to the overall success. This hands-on experience allowed me to see the bigger picture and build a strong foundation in the industry.

From the inception of a design idea to sourcing competitively priced fine fabrics and then arranging preliminary designs on a mannequin to bring initial concepts to life, I learned it all.

I became well-versed in pricing strategies, manufacturing processes, and cost management—everything needed to take a garment from raw fabric to a finished product ready for retail.

Each day, I opened and managed the showroom in the morning. Later in the day, navigating the crooked brick sidewalks in high heels, I headed back to the factory. The experience gave me a deep, practical understanding of the fashion industry, laying the foundation for many of my future endeavors.

Success came swiftly, as I honed a refined and strategic approach to dealing with notoriously tough retail buyers. This skill set was deeply rooted in techniques I'd absorbed from my days with Betty Kraus. Armed with Betty's savvy and a fierce determination, I was prepared for the battlefield, and a battlefield it was!

The wholesale clothing business in 1980's Los Angeles was not for the faint of heart. It was a world dominated by cutthroat and relentless individuals. The intensity began the moment I drove into the parking garage, with cars jockeying for position, cutting each other off in a frenzied rush to be the first to claim a spot. The air was thick with tension, and the competition was palpable.

As my career took off, I developed a refined and effective approach to working with tough retail buyers, thanks to all the Betty techniques I honed.

Around this time, the distance grew between Michael and me and became more apparent. He was content with the status quo, while I was coming into my own, developing ideas and goals I felt were worth pursuing. However, Michael wouldn't budge from his rigid notions. His stubbornness was never more evident than when we began considering the purchase of our first property.

I yearned for a small house, craving the independence and privacy that only a home could offer. Michael, on the other hand, was adamant we only consider a condo. I was tired of apartment-style living, with shared walls and a lack of personal space, and I strongly believed that investing in a house was the smarter financial move.

I tried to show him that, with all things considered, the costs could be the same, but he wouldn't hear it. His refusal to consider my perspective was frustrating. The value of owning a home has proven itself time and again, a truth that's evident in my life today.

Things had shifted between us, and it was clear that my personal growth was at the heart of it. Michael wasn't willing to acknowledge my contributions to the business or the changes I had undergone. When I asked him why the affection between us had faded, his response cut deep: "You drive it out of me." It became clear that he couldn't tolerate my independent thinking, and that was slowly unraveling our relationship.

Michael's stubbornness extended to every aspect of our life together. He was so controlling and tight with budgets that he would never allow me to purchase any of the things I was promoting all day and if I bought anything, he would dismiss my requests with, "Take it back, McCormack," as if speaking to an assistant. This cold detachment only grew, and soon, I was sleeping on the sofa, a mere roommate of the man I once loved so deeply. The worst part was that he had no problem with it. Our separation, though quiet, was profound, and it continued like this for nearly a year.

Blockaded by his stubbornness and my headstrong unwillingness to pull back from my grand, sometimes childish ambitions, there was no path forward. The thought of purchasing property or having children together felt impossible, as either would only complicate matters further. Our dreams no longer aligned, and the tension between my desires and his resistance became too great to overcome. With great sadness, I made the difficult decision and filed for divorce, knowing it was the only way to move forward.

CHAPTER 8

SEEKING SOLACE: A SHIKSA'S SEARCH FOR MEANING

AFTER MY DIVORCE, I EMBARKED ON A LONG, NEVER-satisfying, aimless search for contentment and happiness. I mingled at lavish Beverly Hills parties, jumping from the Mary Pickford Estate to private country clubs, rubbing shoulders with Robert Redford and Sylvester Stallone and other famous stars. I met many well-established men and women and increasingly felt like an outsider navigating a world in which I didn't belong.

In Los Angeles, it was nearly impossible for a shiksa—a gentile woman—like me to find meaningful connections. The Jewish community, where I often interacted, seemed closed off to me. Most of the men I met were divorced and had already built their families. They weren't interested in starting anew, especially not with someone outside their faith. Their lives didn't leave room for the connection and future I longed for. I dated many Jewish men, but it seemed they were not interested in starting a family with a gentile woman. As each year passed, I felt the pressure of my childbearing years slipping away, leaving me increasingly disillusioned and yearning for something that seemed perpetually out of reach.

In hindsight, it was a complete and utter waste of time dating in Los Angeles. I was trying to force something that would never work, battling an unspoken religious barrier that made any real connection nearly impossible. The more I pushed against it, the more counterintuitive it felt, as if I were swimming against a current that constantly pulled me further away from what I truly wanted, a man to share my life with.

My contentment was never truly found in Los Angeles. Life became a series of professional endeavors, moving from one position to the next. I took positions in real estate and financial businesses, including at the Capital Group, which managed American Funds, and Dataquick, a real estate database service similar to today's Zillow and Redfin.

However, securing other jobs often proved challenging without a degree, as most employers required verification from the university. Despite spending a couple of years at UCLA, I never graduated. That didn't stop me from overstating the truth on applications and resumes to convey what was necessary, sometimes stating more than what was strictly true to make the most of the situation.

Fortunately, my mother and I remained close, and although she visited California often, I missed my family deeply. Then, something truly shocking came to light in far-away St. Louis.

• • •

The shock came courtesy of my sister, Mary. After picking up the phone to make a call, she overheard a conversation between Aunt Mary and my stepfather, Wayne. The conversation was far from casual—it was an intimate exchange that revealed a secret relationship between them. And this call wasn't a one-time event. They talked regularly. As their calls continued, it became undeniable that they were secretly involved for most of my mother's marriage.

The revelation was profoundly disturbing, especially for my mother, who began to piece together the troubling signs she long ignored. The mysterious pink lipstick that occasionally appeared suddenly made painful sense. Aunt Mary, who discarded her chance with Wayne seventeen years earlier, now desperately wanted him back—particularly now that his financial stature had risen, with three privately owned grocery stores to his name. The betrayal unraveled a hidden chapter of deceit within our family. If only it had been anyone else—but my mother's own sister? How could my mother's own sister ever reconcile after such a betrayal, especially as it went on for so many years?

My mother and Wayne divorced shortly after, and my mother and sister made the move to Los Angeles. The timing was perfect, as I'd only recently divorced Michael. Having them with me brought a much-needed sense of family and comfort. Both my mother and sister had successfully bought and sold distressed properties in St. Louis, and they were determined to replicate that business in Los Angeles.

Friends and acquaintances, however, were quick to voice their doubts. "This is L.A.," they said. "What worked in St. Louis won't cut it here. The competition will eat you alive." Despite the naysayers, Mom and Mary remained undeterred. The challenges of the Los Angeles market didn't intimidate them; rather, it fueled their resolve. They saw not just a city of stars, but a landscape ripe with opportunity, and they were ready to prove everyone wrong. Their move was more than a new beginning for them—it was a testament to their grit and determination to succeed in a city that many believed would swallow them whole.

After the divorce, Mom received a substantial settlement and used it to buy her first L.A. properties. She and Mary assembled a strong team, but I wasn't included. There was always an undercurrent of competition between us, and this venture was no different. They kept their business closed off from me, a clear signal that I wasn't part of their plans.

It felt like I should offer whatever resources I had to help them, but they never extended the same support to me. I tried to rise above it, accepting that this was how things would be, but their sense of entitlement and selfishness was hard to ignore. It was always present, a constant reminder of the imbalance in our relationships.

In a few months, they were riding the wave of success. My sister, barely in her twenties, became a multi-millionaire, fueled by the vibrant energy of Los Angeles and her new marriage to a nice fellow she'd met, who came from a family of successful real estate investors. Their union was the perfect blend of ambition and opportunity, propelling them forward into a prosperous future.

Together, Mary and Mom were acquiring large, beautiful properties, their future gleaming with promise. Or so it seemed.

Beneath the surface, the dichotomy in their lives was glaring. My sister, despite her newfound wealth, drank far too much and neglected crucial responsibilities like paying her share of taxes. It was as if the faster she climbed, the more precarious her footing became.

While I was dealing with my own issues, my mother, on the other hand, retreated into herself. Once an ambitious, driven woman when Wayne was by her side, she now appeared content to step back, allowing my sister to take the reins of the business exclusively. It was ironic to see my sister, so young and seemingly unstoppable, taking over, while my mother—once the backbone of our family's success—faded into the background. The contrast between their outward successes and underlying issues was a stark reminder that all that glitters isn't gold. As my sister soared, I struggled with my own path, watching from the sidelines as our family dynamics shifted in ways I hadn't anticipated.

Back in St. Louis, Wayne had remarried a woman named Carol, who bore a striking resemblance to my mother—a nearly identical twin. However, Carol had her own struggles, particularly with alcohol, which seemed a recurring curse in my family. It was both ironic and tragic that after all those years, Aunt Mary didn't manage to "slay the dragon" and win Wayne for herself. In the end, whatever they had shared fizzled out into nothing, and they never spoke again.

Wayne's life, though seemingly prosperous, was far from content. His business had expanded to include three or four independent grocery stores, a testament to his hard work and ambition. Yet, his personal life was far from fulfilling. Carol's drinking had become an obsession, leading to unpredictable mood swings that left Wayne increasingly unhappy. To add to his woes, unions were aggressively challenging his business, stirring up legal troubles that threatened to undermine everything he'd built. The juxtaposition of his outward success and inner turmoil was a stark reflection of the price paid when personal and professional lives clash in such devastating ways.

By the age of forty-three, the consequences of Wayne's life choices began catching up with him in ways he could no longer escape. Driven by ambition, he had always pushed the limits, but it seemed he had flown too close to the sun. He frequently joked, almost prophetically, that stomach cancer would be his downfall, and tragically, it was this very illness that ultimately claimed his life.

When we received the news, the family gathered and flew back to see Wayne on his deathbed. It was a profoundly painful experience to watch someone so young, so full of potential, slip away. It wasn't supposed to end like that for Wayne—his life, once brimming with promise, now reduced to a series of unfortunate choices. His infidelity, his years of living a lie, and the weight of unrelenting stress had taken their toll, leading him down a path he couldn't escape. All of these factors converged, ultimately contributing to his untimely death. The loss was devastating, not just because of what he could have been, but because of the self-inflicted wounds that marred his final years.

After Wayne passed, all of his assets were left to our half-sister, Regina. Despite my efforts to reach out and offer a hand of family and connection, we haven't spoken since. Regina and I had never been particularly close, due to our twelve-year age difference and the fact that I left home when she was very young. It's possible that the sudden inheritance shifted her perspective, creating a divide that made it easier for her to distance herself. In doing so, she may have missed the opportunity to embrace a bond that offered something far more enduring than material wealth.

• • •

As my sister's real estate efforts flourished, Mary set her sights on expanding beyond Los Angeles. San Diego, with its picturesque coastline and promising market, became her next target. She rented an executive apartment in Del Mar, ostensibly to transition her business operations there, but it soon became clear that this move had another purpose.

Del Mar offered a sanctuary, a place where Mary could escape the pressures of her burgeoning empire and the strains of her marriage. Behind the allure of this coastal retreat lay a more troubling reality—my sister's growing dependence on alcohol. The apartment, nestled away from prying eyes, provided the perfect cover to indulge in secrecy, far from the scrutiny of her husband and the business world that demanded so much of her.

Sadly, in seeking refuge, Mary was also retreating further, isolating herself from those who cared most for her.

In the 1980s, the contrast between Los Angeles and San Diego was striking. Los Angeles featured a sprawling metropolis, congested streets, and cluttered beaches that often felt overwhelming and chaotic. In contrast, San Diego was a breath of fresh air—quieter, more serene, and distinctly less populated. Del Mar, in particular, stood out as a hidden gem, with its private, affordable neighborhoods and pristine, uncluttered stretches of beach. There, the coastline remained unspoiled, a stark difference from the urban sprawl of L.A.

As we spent more time in San Diego, the allure of its peaceful environment became undeniable. My sisters, my mother, and I were drawn to the area, visiting frequently until we made the decision to relocate there.

Despite the dysfunction and complexities that often defined our family dynamics, there was an unspoken commitment to one another—a deep-seated belief in the importance of family. We intentionally chose to stay close, to bond, to build a life together in this new place. San Diego, with its quieter pace and natural beauty, became not just a refuge from the demands of Los Angeles but a symbol of our commitment to one another.

My mother, the self-proclaimed patron saint of our family, was on a restless mission to discover the true purpose of her life. Her journey led her through a variety of religious experiences, each a different chapter in her search for meaning. She explored the teachings of several churches, from the prosperity gospel of Robert Schuller at the Crystal Cathedral to more unconventional paths. In her spiritual wandering, she even got sucked into a cult that took control of her checkbook, a clear sign of how deeply Mom was searching for answers. Her quest for spiritual fulfillment was intense, reflecting a deep desire to find a guiding light amid the complexities of life.

As my mother searched for spiritual meaning, I grew increasingly disillusioned with California and my own life. Nine years following my divorce, I realized I was chasing something elusive, something I could never quite grasp. Happiness seemed perpetually out of reach, and I couldn't put my finger on what was missing.

California reflected my inner dissatisfaction. The people around me felt shallow and insubstantial, their personalities like modern art rendered in pastel watercolors—visually appealing but lacking depth. This superficiality was mirrored in the design of the homes that dotted the state, whether grand and luxurious or modest and small. I often joked that all the homes in California were just boxes in different sizes, nothing more.

That sentiment was telling—it was easy to critique the emptiness I saw around me, yet far harder to recognize and address the void within myself. Lacking a formal education that could have equipped me to properly assess my strengths and weaknesses against my peers, I was aimless, unsure of where I fit socially. This uncertainty compounded my restlessness, leaving me adrift in a world where appearances reigned, but connection and purpose felt perpetually out of reach.

By 1988, my sister had deftly secured a builder's closeout in Rancho Bernardo and acquired the final seven condominiums in the development, showcasing her astute real estate acumen. Meanwhile, I grappled with a career in real estate marked by inconsistent income and a desire for greater stability. A string of successful closings that summer provided a momentary reprieve, presenting a unique opportunity to pivot towards a new direction.

• • •

I yearned for a setting rich in history and authenticity, far removed from the palm-draped landscapes of California. I was drawn to a region characterized by majestic oak trees and rugged, untamed beaches—an environment that promised depth and cultural resonance. The allure of such a vibrant and genuine place beckoned me, compelling me to explore new horizons and embrace a fresh chapter in my life.

My time spent watching Arthur Fiedler and the Boston Pops with Michael Adachi had sparked a deep fascination with the Kennedy legacy, Martha's Vineyard, and our country's esteemed Ivy League institutions. The allure of New England's rich history and academic prestige resonated within me, drawing me toward a new chapter. With my financial reserves in place and a well-honed ability to adapt to new environments, I took the opportunity for a fresh start.

The prospect of discovering the historic landscapes of New England and delving into its vibrant cultural fabric excited me. I was ready to take a leap of faith, confident that if my new path didn't unfold as hoped, the option to return remained. It was time to venture beyond the horizon and uncover what lay ahead.

Fueled by a mix of naïveté, enthusiasm, and blind faith, I found myself rekindling a fervor for life and adventure. With a renewed zest for the unknown, I embraced the idea of placing myself on a map without a set plan, allowing faith and serendipity to guide my journey. There was something deeply invigorating about surrendering to possibility, trusting that the uncharted path ahead would lead me to where I was meant to be.

Before taking this leap of faith, I meticulously planned my move. I reached out to small business owners and members of local chambers of commerce to gather insights into the business landscape. I immersed myself in *The Boston Globe*, thoroughly researching real estate values in the most affluent neighborhoods where I envisioned myself living and working. My criteria included low crime rates—a practically redundant consideration, given Boston's reputation for safety among major U.S. cities—and proximity to exclusive designer shops and pristine, rugged coastlines.

The promise of discovering new friendships and finding a supportive community further ignited my excitement. Who would I meet? Who would I become? Only time would tell.

PHOTOS

A PICTORIAL JOURNEY

FORMER CONVICT IS ARRESTED IN MYSZAK KILLING

Elmer (Jack) McCormack Booked Suspected of Murder— Is Friend of Spica.

Elmer (Jack) McCormack, a former convict, was arrested by St. Louis county police today for questioning in the investigation of the John J. Myszak killing. He was booked suspected of first degree murder.

Police said that McCormack was a friend of John Paul Spica, a hoodlum who is being held on a murder warrant. McCormack, 38 years old, has been arrested many times since 1941 for investigation of automobile theft, robbery, burglary, larceny and arson. He lives in the 5600 block of Pershing avenue.

McCormack was released after about two hours and was turned over to Wellston police who said he would be questioned in a burglary investigation.

Chief of Detectives F. J. (Pete) Vasel, who is directing the Myszak murder investigation, questioned Spica extensively again today. He declined to say what Spica told him. Two other ex-convicts were arrested in the investigation but were released after being questioned.

Myszak, St. Louis county real estate operator, was shot to death June 8 when standing in the driveway of a client's home at 915 Bermuda drive, Normandy.

Vasel said that he and Detective Sgt. Glennon B. Kirchhoff will appear before the county

By a Post-Dispatch Photographer.

Held in County

ELMER (JACK) McCORMACK

grand jury next week to give detailed information about their investigation of the murder.

Myszak's 48-year-old widow, the only witness called before the grand jury so far, will not be asked to give further testimony, Vasel said. She testified for two hours last Tuesday under questioning by Prosecuting Attorney Norman H. Anderson.

Spica, who denied any knowledge of the Myszak murder, will be given a preliminary hearing next Thursday in the court of Magistrate Peter J. Maniscalco at Clayton.

County detectives arrested Spica Monday night in front of Mrs. Myszak's home at 3671 Manola avenue, Uplands Park Village. Spica had received $1000 in marked bills from the widow just before the arrest, police said.

St. Louis Post-Dispatch,
July 20, 1962

FORMER CONVICT HELD AS 'BRAINS' IN BUSCH HOLDUP

Other Suspects Say Normandy Man Planned $17,200 Robbery of Credit Union.

Elmer Otto McCormack, an ex-convict, was arrested today by police and charged by Circuit Attorney Daniel P. Reardon Jr. with being the "brains" of the $17,200 Anheuser-Busch credit union robbery Aug. 3.

Reardon issued a warrant charging McCormack with armed robbery. McCormack, 37 years old, was arrested by county police at his home in the 3900 block of Cranberry lane, Normandy, and was brought to St. Louis Police Headquarters.

The circuit attorney said that participants in the robbery told him that McCormack planned the holdup and outlined how it should be handled. The associates said that McCormack made two or three visits to the credit union office at 1046 South Broadway to "case" the job.

Three men had been arrested previously for participating in the holdup and two have admitted their part.

Reardon quoted those who have confessed as saying that McCormack met with them at several secret places to go over the plans.

McCormack, who denied having any connection with holdup, already is under bond on a charge of being the leader of an automobile theft ring that cut up stolen cars and sold the parts. He is also charge with receiving stolen property.

Donald Ray Lindsey, one of the suspects in the Anheuser-Busch robbery, is scheduled to be returned to St. Louis tomorrow from Pasadena, Calif., where he was arrested last week. He had more than $2000 in his possession when arrested.

The men admitting their part in the robbery are Thomas S. Carter, ex-convict, of the 1800 block of Stockard avenue, Maplewood, and Samuel Rudolph Handley, of the 7900 block of West Bruno avenue, Maplewood. Police have recovered about $5000 of the loot.

St. Louis Post-Dispatch,
August 13, 1962

FORMER CONVICT, FIGURE IN BUSCH ROBBERY, KILLED

Elmer (Jack) McCormack, Under Indictment, Is Shot to Death in Wellston.

Elmer O. (Jack) McCormack, an ex-convict, was shot and killed today by Louis Wallach, former boxing promoter and operator of an automobile salvage company.

The shooting occurred in the office of Wallach's firm, the Harlan Salvage Co., 1604 Lucas-Hunt road, Wellston.

Although Wallach said he fired in self defense when McCormack attempted to hold him up, he was arrested by Wellston police and booked suspected of homicide.

McCormack, 38 years old, had been charged with being the "brains" of the $17,500 robbery of the Anheuser-Busch credit union office last Aug. 3. He was under indictment for first-degree robbery.

Assistant Prosecuting Attorney Daniel O'Brien of St. Louis county said that Wallach told him McCormack came to his salvage company about 11 a.m.

Room Dimly Lit.

"Wallach said he was standing in the office, a converted garage," O'Brien told a reporter. "The room was dimly lit and Wallach was about 10 feet to the right of the doorway.

"Wallach said he heard someone say, 'This is a stickup; I want the money.' He said he did not turn around, but reached slowly for a drawer of a metal filing cabinet in which there was a revolver."

O'Brien quoted Wallach as saying he picked up the weapon, spun around and fired three times in the direction of the voice. All three bullets struck McCormack.

Shot in Heart, Eye, Shoulder.

McCormack was shot in the heart, under the right eye and in one shoulder.

Wallach telephoned the Wellston police station. Cpl. Roger Spreck, who answered the call, said when he drove up Wallach was standing in the doorway with the revolver in his hand.

What's the trouble?" Spreck asked.

"I just shot a burglar,"

Continued on Page 7, Col. 2.

Figures in Killing

LOUIS WALLACH, in police car after shooting.

Former Convict

Continued From Page One.

Wallach replied.

Pagedale and county police and Coroner Raymond I. Harris went to the scene. Police found no weapon on McCormack's body or near the place where he was lying. The body was behind a counter, some distance from the door.

Most of the students attending classes in Normandy High School, across the street were unaware of the shooting. A few students standing on the sidewalk had heard the shots.

McCormack's automobile was parked on a lot in front of the building.

Wallach told Coroner Harris that he and McCormack had engaged in a number of business transactions in the past. They bought and sold automobile parts to each other, Wallach said.

ELMER (JACK) McCORMACK

"I told McCormack I didn't want anything more to do with him," Wallach told Harris. "McCormack had been ordered to stay out of Wellston. Last Thursday evening he dropped by my house in the 1100 block of Backer avenue, University City, where my wife and I were celebrating our twenty-fifth wedding anniversary."

Wallach said that McCormack paid a brief visit to his home last night.

Wallach was held without bond by Wellston police, who also took an employe of the salvage company into custody. The employe, John Franks, of the 5700 block of Horlamont avenue, was held as a material witness. He told police that he was working in a junk yard behind the office when the shooting occurred.

McCormack, who lived in the 3900 block of Cranberry lane, Normandy, had been charged with being the head of a ring which cut up stolen automobiles and sold the parts. A charge of receiving stolen property was pending against him.

Arrested Many Times.

Last July McCormack was arrested and held for questioning in the murder of John J. Myszak, St. Louis county real estate dealer. He has been arrested many times since 1941 for investigation of automobile theft, robbery, burglary, larceny and arson, and in 1946 received a five-year federal sentence for theft of automobile tires from interstate shipment.

Wallach was implicated by Robert Earl Barnes, a burglar, with being a "fence" for burglary loot. Wallach was convicted of receiving stolen property and was sentenced to one year in prison, but won a new trial. A jury found him not guilty of the charge last May after Barnes refused to testify a second time.

Police said McCormack was at county police headquarters in Clayton about 30 minutes before the shooting. They did not disclose what he was doing there.

St. Louis Post-Dispatch,
October 29, 1962

LOUIS WALLACH IS ARRESTED ON MURDER CHARGE

Indicted in Killing of Associate, Jack McCormack — Held Without Bond.

Louis Wallach, Wellston auto parts dealer and former boxing promoter, was arrested today on a first degree murder indictment. He was taken to jail at Clayton and will be held without bond.

Wallach was indicted Dec. 4 by the St. Louis county grand jury in the killing of an associate, Elmer O. (Jack) McCormack, a former convict. The indictment was suppressed until today when Wallach answered on a $10,000 appearance bond before Magistrate Peter J. Maniscalco at Clayton. After Wallach was discharged on the bond, a deputy sheriff served a copy of indictment and made the arrest.

Wallach has admitted that he shot McCormack on Oct. 29 at the Harlan Salvage Co., which he operates at 1604 Lucas-Hunt road. He insisted that he fired in self-defense when McCormack tried to hold him up.

Wallach told police he had broken off business relations with McCormack, who was under indictment in the $17,000 Anheuser-Busch Credit Union robbery.

However, Wellston police learned that the two men had many dealings in the purchase and sale of automobile parts and that McCormack was a frequent visitor at the salvage company.

Parts for late-model cars, valued at thousands of dollars, were found, with three partly dismantled stolen cars, in the yard behind Wallach's salvage office. Police concluded that the junkyard was used by a gang of thieves as a place for cutting up stolen cars.

Investigators concluded that McCormack was suspected by some of his associates of passing information about them to county authorities. The suspicions may have led to the shooting of McCormack, the Post-Dispatch learned.

St. Louis Post-Dispatch,
December 13, 1962

My father, Jack McCormack.

My father, Jack McCormack, holding me.

Grandpa Roy, me, Nana (above).
Grandpa Roy and Nana (right).

Aunt Mary beside Nana,
who sat in her tub chair,
wearing pearls.

Showing my shy side in the center of this photo, taken with my great grandmother.

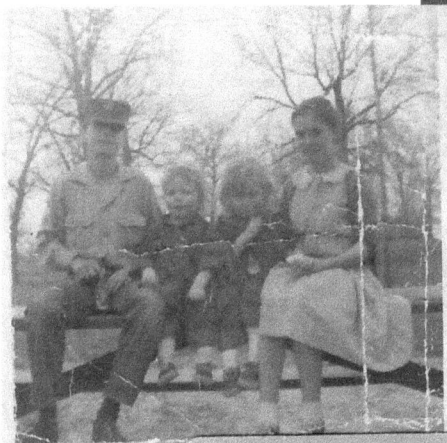

Uncle Billy and Aunt Mary flank me and my sister, Mary.

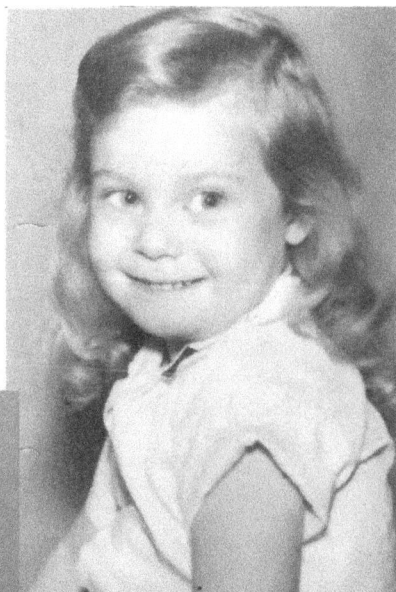

Me (above) and my sister, Mary, and me (left).

Early modeling days.

Modeling in Chicago.

Mom and me in Rhode Island.

Me, Mom, and my sister, Mary in Fort Lauderdale, Florida.

My stepfather, Wayne.

Me and Mike Adachi.

Photos with Rachel in 1993, the happiest year of my life!

Mom and me.

Mom holding me.

Me and Mom at Rachel's dedication.

Rachel growing up.

Rachel dancing in her Quincy Market dress, like usual.

Rachel preparing to
head off to college.

Rachel at
University of
California -
Santa Barbara.

My husband, Dan, me, and our Boxer dog, Avigail.

CHAPTER 9

STORMING BOSTON: A RED MUSTANG, BALI SHOES, A MISSION, AND A HURRICANE

IT WAS AUGUST 15, 1990. AS MY FLIGHT DESCENDED INTO Boston Logan International Airport, a surge of exhilaration coursed through me. The landscape below was a stunning mosaic of green with the Atlantic Ocean gleaming to the right. Through the window, my future seemed to take shape, cherished and waiting to unfold. Breathless with anticipation, my thoughts raced—where would this new journey lead? What extraordinary experiences lay ahead?

By the time I wrangled my enormous suitcase and rented a fiery red convertible Mustang, the sun was well below the horizon. Plunging into unfamiliar darkness made navigating Massachusetts roads— roads that evolved from ancient, winding cow paths—daunting. I was armed with a well-worn paper map, folded into six sections, and vague directions from the airport parking attendant as I began the journey toward Ipswich, my heart pounding with a mix of excitement and trepidation.

Heading north, my anxiety of getting lost crept in. I made a quick stop at a gas station to ask a kind-faced gentleman for directions. His thick South Boston accent made his words almost indecipherable, as he made repeated mention of going around the "rotary." Signs for rotaries were everywhere, yet the meaning remained elusive—what was a rotary, and why was it so significant? It all felt like a puzzle, the first of many that Massachusetts had in store for me.

Sensing my confusion and utter lack of direction, the man took pity on me.

He gave a warm, reassuring smile and offered to lead the way. Relieved, I followed his car through the maze of unfamiliar roads, grateful for his unexpected kindness. He guided me all the way to my turnoff, transforming what could have been a harrowing detour into a small, comforting adventure.

The quiet, private gravel road leading to my bed-and-breakfast destination looked like a serene passage through a storybook. The road, softly illuminated by the glow of garden lights and the warm radiance of the innkeeper's porch light, guided me to a sweet country inn on that gentle, waning August evening.

The air was balmy, and the soothing symphony of crickets greeted my arrival. At that moment, fatigue gave way to profound relief. I'd conquered the first leg of my journey and was enveloped in a sense of peace and anticipation for the exciting week ahead. The tranquil scene seemed a comforting omen, a promising restful haven, the beginning of a memorable adventure.

The following morning, I donned my sleek, understated black V-neck sheath dress, elegantly cinched at the waist. Paired with my pristine black leather Bali pumps—never before worn—and gold watch, pearl necklace, and polished leather attaché, I felt poised and refined. Climbing into my Mustang, I set off to visit Vera Taylor at Fox Hill Village, ready to embrace the day's possibilities with style and grace.

My drive to Westwood brought a revelation. It was as if I had entered a living kaleidoscope of colors and textures that starkly contrasted the muted hues of Southern California. The landscape unfolded in rich, verdant shades, with flowers blooming naturally in a riot of colors, and large, billowing trees towering over well-mannered shrubs. The sky, a canvas of the most exquisite blues, was occasionally brushed with soft, drifting clouds. The air was crisp and fragrant with the scent of clover, wrapping me in a refreshing embrace that made me feel truly alive. In that moment, it was as if I had discovered a slice of paradise, a breathtaking haven that breathed new life into my senses.

As I approached the handsome circular driveway, I was greeted by a picturesque display of vibrant gardens flanking the grand porte cochère. Fox Hill Village seamlessly integrated into a residential neighborhood, where stately older homes stood as testaments to a bygone era of architectural magnificence. The enchanting scene was a harmonious blend of nature and sophistication that welcomed me with open arms.

My arrival was met with a warm reception at the front desk, and the ambiance exuded the refined elegance of an upscale hotel. I waited in the lobby for the staff to escort me to my interview, taking in the surroundings. The sophistication of the setting, paired with my sleek blonde chignon, pearls, and effortlessly chic Bali shoes, put me at ease.

The entire experience was a seamless blend of luxury and grace, perfectly aligning with the image I had envisioned.

The position I hoped to secure involved selling luxurious real estate tailored to affluent seniors, focusing particularly on upscale, hotel-style accommodations. Fox Hill Village, which I assumed was the property in question, was a prestigious development resulting from a partnership between Hillhaven and Mass General Hospital. The elegant apartments commanded substantial entrance fees, ranging from approximately $300,000 to over $1 million with monthly fees of $4,000 to $7,000 for the first resident, and more for a second occupant.

I understood the importance of "leaning in at the interview, asking questions and showing genuine interest. It was easy—I truly was intrigued. I could have easily envisioned myself living among those residents. To make my vision reality, I employed all my polished sales techniques, channeling my inner Betty Kraus. Ultimately, my connection with Vera sealed the deal. We clicked effortlessly, as if the stars had aligned on our behalf and we were destined to be best friends. Everything about my trip felt imbued with a sense of providence, as if the stars had aligned perfectly to make this moment auspicious.

Less than a week after my interview, Vera reached out to present an exciting opportunity with the Hillhaven Corporation. The role was not directly with Fox Hill Village; rather, it involved working for a "sister" community in Walpole, Massachusetts, just a few miles away. Vera emphasized the urgent need for someone to assist with the preconstruction phase of this new senior community, which was—at the time—represented only by an architectural rendering and a model of a one-bedroom unit.

This position came with a competitive salary, commissions, annual bonuses, and excellent benefits. It was a valuable opportunity to showcase my enthusiasm, sales skills, and personal affinity for working with the elderly and the affluent, aligning perfectly with my professional goals and passions.

Naturally, I accepted the offer—who wouldn't? The opportunity seemed almost too good to be true. I began my new role immediately, only to find that Walpole was a stark departure from the refined charm I had envisioned. Unlike Westwood's affluence and cultural sophistication, Walpole's demographic leaned more blue-collar, reflecting its roots in a working-class community. The area around the retirement community was less polished than anticipated; its proximity to a landfill, a recycling center, and most jarring of all, the State Prison, painted a picture far from the idyllic setting I imagined for an upscale retirement experience.

While I was determined to succeed, it was clear that the clientele and environment would pose challenges I hadn't anticipated.

Lacking the full suite of resources to convey my message through conversation and correspondence, I immersed myself in the community's literature and brochures with fervent dedication. These professionally crafted materials became my primary tools. By memorizing their content and delivering it verbatim to hundreds of prospects over the phone, I aimed to accomplish the extraordinary. My task was selling a concept that existed only in theoretical images, as the actual product was neither present nor tangible. It was a formidable challenge—talk about a hard sell! Not to mention its less-than-ideal surroundings. But I was dedicated, eager to prove to myself and my new employer that I had what it took to find success.

I was lonely and like my clientele, eager to make friends. A clever sense of humor became my bridge to connection. "Walpole?" potential clients asked. "Why on earth would I want to move to Walpole?" In my heart of hearts, I agreed. Say it out loud—Walpole! Doesn't it sound comically absurd? But their questions didn't end there. "What about the landfill? And, oh dear, the State Prison!" Those were tough questions to dodge. I couldn't make them disappear or pretend those unsavory sites weren't part of the landscape. How do you glamorize a town where the highlight is the view of a landfill and a state prison? It was an uphill battle, to say the least!

But I fought, and I pulled off the impossible. Here's how I did it.

"Mrs. Sullivan," I told a potential client with typical questions, "let me be honest—I've driven every street in Walpole and, truthfully, I've never seen that landfill. As for the prison, well, think about it. If you escaped from the Walpole State Prison, where would you go? Not back to Walpole, that's for sure! You'd be heading as far away as possible to avoid getting caught. So, Mrs. Sullivan, trust me, Walpole's not the place to be worried about. In fact, it's probably the safest."

"Perhaps you should come over to take a look at our model apartment. It might surprise you." This line often caught their attention, offering a peek into the luxury and comfort they could experience, even in an area that didn't initially meet their expectations. Once I had their interest, I would dive deeper, guiding them toward the next step.

"Now," I'd continue, "let's talk about something more exciting—when can you come for a visit? Do you have your calendar handy? I'm happy to wait while you fetch it. Which day works best for you, Tuesday or Friday next week? I'm positively thrilled at the thought of meeting you!"

With this tactic, my sales numbers were solid, and I kept copious notes on every prospect. I knew corporate read everything I documented, so I kept my trusty *Roget's Thesaurus* and *Webster's Dictionary* on my desk. Turns out, I was a hit in Massachusetts—they couldn't get enough of the blonde from California. They never let me forget why I'd moved to the cold Northeast, pointing out that most people headed in the opposite direction. I joked with them that I was banking on global warming and soon, New England winters would be the new hot spot! They'd laugh, and it was fun bringing humor into the mix whenever I could. I'd even preach that I adored children and the elderly because they were "closer" to God—there's just an innocent presence in both.

I was knocking it out of the ballpark, even managing to close sales in the heart of winter. And oh, that first winter—I was captivated! Snow draped over every inch of Walpole, transforming even mundane landscape into a picturesque fairyland. While my colleagues were weighed down by the relentless cold and gloom, often expressing tremendous dread, I couldn't help but marvel at the serene beauty of it all. My sense of humor and upbeat outlook lifted their spirits, even when they struggled to find joy in the season. Corporate was very happy with their choice.

After sharing a house in Cohasset, that spring I rented a townhome at 131 Glades Road in Scituate, a forty-minute drive to work. Scituate awakened my senses in ways I hadn't experienced before. The thought of being by the ocean every day was irresistible. This South Shore community on Massachusetts Bay was just south of Boston and offered everything I imagined and more.

The first thing that embraced me was the fresh scent of the ocean air, which seemed to wrap around me the moment I arrived. It carried the unmistakable essence of the abundant fish below the surface, a subtle reminder of the rich marine life that thrived just beyond the shore.

Then there was the nearly seamless stretch of transparent grey, where the sea met the sky in a hazy, indistinguishable line on cloud-covered days, offering a profound sense of calm and solitude. This cloud-induced tranquility was only occasionally disrupted by the gentle lapping of water against the jagged coastline and the distant cries of seagulls gliding overhead.

At the end of the jetty, the iconic Minot Beach Lighthouse stood proudly, a historic beacon for sailors and fishing boats. Walking paths along the water and through the quaint, nonconforming cape houses were some of the finest I've ever seen. Each house had its own distinctive personality, as unique as the people who lived in them. The place captivated my senses and my soul.

Did I mention how much I loved Scituate? How much I adored my terrific job? Golly, I was in heaven! Everything seemed to align perfectly—this charming coastal town, the vibrant energy of my work, it all felt like a dream come true.

But I wanted more. There's always more happiness to be had, right? Isn't this the essence of the human experience?

• • •

Riding high on the wave of a well-earned bonus, I decided it was time to treat myself. So, off I went to Copley Plaza and Newbury Street, where the most refined and cutting-edge designer shops beckoned. Chanel, Celine of Paris, Dior, Fendi, Gucci—the names alone were intoxicating. Newbury Street was a haven of exclusivity, with boutique after boutique offering increasingly luxurious finds, each store more refined than the last, drawing me deeper into a world of high-end fashion and sophistication.

I was swept up in the experience, trying on five different pairs of exquisite Italian leather shoes without even a glance at the price tags. Convinced I deserved them all, I took all five pairs, feeling like a princess who had just completed her coronation. That weekend, I returned to my seaside haven in Scituate, arms laden with bundles of clothing and shoes—a lifetime of pent-up desire to own something truly mine, finally fulfilled.

But then, something unexpected happened. Standing in the stillness of my room, surrounded by my exquisite treasures, I felt . . . nothing. The joy I so eagerly anticipated, the rush of satisfaction I expected to wash over me, eluded me. It was as if the excitement drained away the moment those bags touched the floor. For the first time, I was confronted with an unsettling paradox that ran contrary to everything I believed: being surrounded with an abundance of beautiful things did not guarantee joy. Not even a flicker. In that moment, I realized with startling clarity that happiness—true, lasting happiness—was not something that could be conjured up by material things. At least not for me.

I did love my work, though, and my commitment was evident in every detail. I meticulously curated a wardrobe of fifteen suits, each in a different hue that spanned the entire spectrum of the rainbow. My efforts ensured I always looked the part—poised, articulate, and the definitive ambassador of New Pond Village of Walpole.

Corporate recognized my dedication and rewarded me with the best office in the building. I adorned it with fine art from local galleries and infused the space with a subtle touch of fragrance from a diffuser. I even invested in my first word processor, the Brother WP-2400—a rather cumbersome beige box that was allegedly portable, though at twenty pounds, it was something of an albatross to carry around.

My dedication to my work was unwavering, and it was clearly paying off.

On my calendar, a prominent memo reminded me to "Remember Betty Kraus"—a tribute to my enduring mentor, many years after I left her side. In May of 1991, Hillhaven Corporation celebrated the grand opening of a brand-new building with a formal ribbon-cutting ceremony. After months of dedication and hard work, my team and the staff finally saw New Pond Village come to life, ready to welcome residents.

At one point, the Hillhaven Corporation incentivized us with a generous bonus—twice our salaries—if we achieved a specific number of move-ins. Initially, there was a powerful drive among my colleagues, but as time went on, enthusiasm began to wane. I worked late into the evening, often the only person in the office, determined to meet the company's goals and uphold the vision we worked so hard to realize.

• • •

Selling at New Pond Village was far more than leasing apartments; it was about facilitating a comprehensive continuum of care that combined the elegance of a fine hotel with exceptional amenities.

The process often involved navigating complex family dynamics and delicate issues.

One particularly challenging case involved a renowned doctor who wished to move in with his companion, only to face strong opposition from his family. The situation necessitated private family meetings, which frequently became quite heated. My role was to act as a mediator in these skirmishes, maintaining an impartial stance while striving to bring harmony to both sides and ultimately ensuring the best outcome for the couple.

This intricate balancing act was not a single transaction but often a series of delicate negotiations, each one unique and surprisingly complex. It was a demanding yet deeply fulfilling experience, one I consider among the most rewarding periods of my career.

In my relentless drive to meet company milestones, I dined with potential clients for lunch and dinner every day. Delicious as it was, the constant eating in the fine dining rooms made me concerned about gaining weight. When my colleagues made a video celebrating our achievements, with a touch of irony I wore a tent dress stuffed with a pillow to humorously represent the extra pounds I accumulated along the way. Looking back, it was a tacit sign of changes to come, though at the time, I was oblivious to the deeper significance behind that humorous portrayal.

On Fridays, I frequented Faneuil Hall and Quincy Market, where history and lively energy mingled seamlessly. On weekends, I often basked in the serene beauty of Cape Cod, the picturesque allure of Newport, Rhode Island, or the peaceful escape of Kennebunkport, Maine. In the summer, I indulged in beach towns, while winters were reserved for the classic New England charm of Concord, New Hampshire, and the snow-capped beauty of Stowe, Vermont. Throughout my travels, I longed to share these experiences with my mother, who was back in San Diego. Despite the complexities in our family dynamics, I would often start weekend calls with, "Hi Mom, guess where I am?" Her voice offered comfort like no other. I missed her and yearned for her to witness and celebrate my accomplishments alongside me in these enchanting places. I missed her so very much.

After my first year in Boston, I felt confident as we were ahead of our goals for New Pond Village. I purchased some lovely furniture from my boss who was moving and shipped my grand piano from storage in San Diego. My apartment looked fabulous, and as my movers were finishing up, my neighbors casually mentioned, "You know, your building has been hit in the past and destroyed by Nor'easters." With a carefree shrug, I jested, "Well, what are the chances?"

October in New England is nothing short of extraordinary. The crisp air fills with the scent of fallen leaves and burning wood, while the landscape transforms into a blazing tapestry of fiery reds and golden yellows. The beauty of the season is intoxicating, and I immersed myself in it fully, even taking horseback riding lessons surrounded by the stunning foliage.

Despite the beauty, the month of October always carried a shadow—the whisper of something ominous. As Monday, October 28 approached, that familiar sense of foreboding grew stronger. The forecast spoke of a brewing Nor'easter down in Florida, its path tracing the East Coast, threatening to unleash giant disturbances and dangerously high water levels. It felt as if a dark presence was lurking beneath the autumnal charm, a reminder of the painful occurrences that marked past Octobers in my life.

Fear gripped me as I listened to the news. While no one in Walpole seemed concerned—after all, New Pond Village was far inland—I couldn't shake my growing unease. Then, the forecast took a dark turn, with talk of possible evacuations necessary on the coast before Wednesday.

Returning home Tuesday night, I was met with a sight that filled me with dread I had never known. The sea had transformed into a churning mass of dark grey, tinged with a sickly green, and it rose as if driven by an unnatural, malevolent force. It appeared some devilish hand had turned on a faucet, the water pouring in too rapid to comprehend. The ocean seemed to rage against its boundaries, as if warning me to flee from its wrath. The wall that once stood as a barrier against high tides now seemed like a fragile thread, ready to snap at any moment.

High tide was predicted with eerie precision—3:11 p.m. on Wednesday. The time felt like an impending sentence without escape. Despite the fear that gnawed at me, I parked my car and went inside the house, while the sound outside rose to a deafening crescendo, echoing the storm preparing to unleash its full fury.

I wrestled with sleep, haunted by one thought: If the storm breached the wall, would I have enough time to escape to safety? The rain poured relentlessly through the night, each drop a reminder of the impending danger. By morning, my nerves were frayed. I moved with a sense of urgency. I packed an overnight bag with enough clothes for a few days, threw my favorite outfits in the bathtub for safekeeping, closed the closets, and dashed to my car in the pouring rain.

Soon as I threw the car into gear to leave, I realized I was in trouble—my car was stuck, lodged in the mud and rocks, with no traction. I tried everything—starting, stopping, backing up, revving the engine—and nothing worked. Paranoia crept in as I noticed most of my neighbors had already gone. Panic was setting in when suddenly, a cop car appeared out of thin air.

My savior! The officer saw my predicament and came to my rescue. He knew exactly what he was doing. In seconds, he freed my car and backed it onto the road, allowing me to escape before the storm swallowed me whole.

Phew! The hour-long drive to Walpole in the pouring rain was a tense journey, each mile fraught with the anxiety of what lay around the next turn. The relentless downpour mirrored the storm in my mind, which I had to tamper down and focus. I couldn't spend all my brainpower on the rain. I had to mentally prepare for the workday. It was going to be a busy one, with a luncheon at noon, but all the while, I couldn't shake the nagging awareness of the time.

I made it to work and buried myself in the day's tasks. After lunch, I came up for air and called my apartment, just to check. The answering machine clicked on, a small relief, but my unease persisted. Every half hour, I called again, and each time, the machine answered—until 3:10

p.m. At precisely 3:11 p.m., I dialed my number, but this time, the machine was silent. No response. It was dead.

My heart sank, the pit in my stomach growing deeper with each passing second. I feared the worst. The dread of what awaited me at home hung over me like a dark cloud, making the thought of my long drive back unbearable. Anxiety gnawed at me, twisting my thoughts into a tangled mess of fear and uncertainty.

CHAPTER 10

FROM CHAOS TO CREATION: WELCOMING SWEET RACHEL ELIZABETH

THE RAIN FELL IN RELENTLESS SHEETS, POUNDING AGAINST THE car with the intensity of a hurricane. Visibility was near impossible as I leaned closer to the windshield, struggling to navigate through the storm. The torrential downpour mirrored the dread that weighed heavily on my chest, each gust of wind and wall of water amplifying the sense of unease.

As I neared Glades Road, the scene was nothing short of a war zone. Debris scattered across the landscape like the remnants of a life torn asunder. My heart sank further as the reality of the devastation hit me in waves.

Rounding the final corner, I came face to face with the ruins of what was once my home. The house was a mere shell of its former glory, reduced to a skeletal framework clinging to a battered foundation. The roof was gone, the walls ripped apart, leaving an eerie, exposed structure mimicking an abandoned dollhouse left out in the rain. The destruction was total.

Now toppled onto its side, my piano, its once-pristine frame was now swollen and waterlogged—a heartbreaking reflection of the destruction around it. Its presence struck a particularly bitter chord, as my last payments for it were still in view, a haunting reminder of its value to me, both financial and emotional. The piano, which had consoled me in my darkest moments, now stood as a poignant monument to loss, its silent keys echoing the void left in the wake of the storm.

It was beyond saving, a heart-wrenching casualty of the storm. My personal files, years of tax returns, and other carefully kept records of my life's work, had been swept out to sea, vanished without a trace. The appliances were soaked and reduced to useless hunks of metal. What little furniture remained was strewn about, upended, and buried in mud and gravel, tossed by the storm shoving them aside like leaves caught in a violent gust of wind.

Everywhere I looked was loss. The home I so carefully assembled, the life I built within those walls, lay in ruins around me. Yet, amid the devastation, I found a small, bittersweet glimmer of relief. My wardrobe, a collection of carefully chosen pieces that accompanied me on my journey, was miraculously intact, untouched by the chaos that consumed everything else. It was a strange comfort, a reminder that not all was lost, even with such overwhelming destruction. But the sadness lingered, a heavy, inescapable presence, as I stood amid the wreckage of what had once been, struggling to come to terms with the enormity of what was gone.

I knew that finding a new place to live would be a challenge, especially while managing the demands of a stressful job. In the coming days and weeks, my colleagues gave gentle reminders that I was safe, and that was most important. Everything else, they promised, would eventually fall into place. I appreciated their kindness, tightening my lips to keep my heartbreak to myself.

• • •

Despite the success of New Pond Village, a seed of discontent had taken root. I was told I sold myself right out of a job. The statement was meant to praise my achievements, yet it only highlighted the lack of true appreciation for my hard work. Was this really the reward for all my effort?

It seemed a bit perverse if they had asked me, but no one asked my opinion. I felt the close of a chapter was looming, and I felt a deep within me urge to advance to the next level. After more than three years, it was clear that Walpole was not where my future lay, so it was again time to set out to find my future.

With my usual gumption and a hard-hitting response to their innuendo, I didn't wait for an invitation to forge ahead. There was a senior development convention for corporate executives in Denver coming up. A chance to network with industry execs, gain insight into future communities, and enjoy a mountain getaway at the same time? It made perfect sense. Marriott senior executives would be there, and I was determined to talk to them.

As winter dragged on and memories of the No Name Hurricane lingered in the back of my mind, I readied for a change. My Denver plans were still taking shape, but the endless cold and grey of New England were wearing on me.

I decided a long weekend in Fort Lauderdale, Florida, was what I needed. The summer colors, warm sun, and endless sea beckoned, a stark contrast to the chill that had settled over my life. South Florida in winter—especially during spring break—promised a burst of energy and life reminiscent of my dancing days in Los Angeles. It had been far too long since I felt that kind of freedom, that life-giving pulse, and I was more than ready to embrace it.

Breaking away from the routine was liberating. Hundreds of miles from Walpole, with a stunning view of the sea from my window in Delray, Florida, allowed me to carve out a moment of separation before diving back into the demands of life.

The concierge, my trusted ally while traveling, presented a selection of exquisite venues that promised entertainment and indulgence. Exclusive clubs and fine eateries nestled along the canal, where luxurious private yachts glided by in silence, a glimpse into a world of opulence.

After dinner, I lingered for a while, absorbing the deep bass rhythms pulse through the room, resonating not just in the air but within me. The perfectly balanced sound system cast an enchanting spell, its vibrations weaving through the space and tempting me to surrender to the music. It was as if the rhythm itself was alive, calling me to the dance floor with an irresistible energy.

There was just one problem: I didn't have a partner. Yet, the night held an allure, the air filled with the promise of something special, waiting to be embraced.

Finally, a young man, boyish in his slight frame, caught my eye. His unwavering, insistent gaze carried a silent invitation that lingered in the air between us. He didn't back down, and with a subtle, almost daring smile, he extended a hand, gesturing me to the empty dance floor. I glanced around, searching for another offer, a fleeting hesitation in the air, but the moment was clear—this was the chance before me. Take it or leave it.

What did I have to lose? The thought echoed in my mind, reminding me of a jest I once heard: A dance is hardly a marriage proposal. So, why not? The night was young, the music irresistible, and the moment pulled at my desire to dance and cut loose. With a shrug that belied my inner thrill, I let go of my reservations. I wanted to dance—so what the hell?

My partner's remarkable skill in synchronizing rhythm with physical grace captivated me, and I was lost in the sheer joy of it. The song ended, but we continued dancing, and as long as he was willing, I was willing to dance the night away. His youthful exuberance and infectious happiness were irresistible, transforming the evening into a celebration of vitality and mirth. With a terrific dance partner and shared laughter, the night was utterly grand.

As we swept across the dance floor, I learned his name was Christopher Farnsworth. He hailed from Austin, Texas and his rich, deep sonorous voice carried the unmistakable warmth of the South.

When I mentioned that I was living in Boston, his eyes lit up with a spark of curiosity. He'd never been to New England, but he spoke with genuine enthusiasm about the possibility of visiting. As our conversation unfolded, I discovered that Christopher was just twenty-six, twelve years younger than me. With that knowledge, I couldn't take him seriously, but I simply enjoyed the moment.

In a lighthearted gesture, I invited Christopher up to Boston for a weekend in May, just in time for his birthday. To my surprise, he accepted.

As I prepared to leave Fort Lauderdale, I couldn't shake the strange reluctance about parting ways with Christopher, despite barely knowing him. He was so easy to read, so refreshingly free of hidden agendas. His openness and authenticity were disarming, unlike anyone I had ever met. He maintained a high-spirited, positive energy that made him easy to connect with. I was oddly drawn to his unguarded sincerity.

On my way back to the airport, a subtle void began to form, a feeling of emptiness I couldn't quite understand. It lingered in the quiet moments, in the spaces between thoughts, as if hinting at the many departures yet to come. The feeling was unsettling, almost a whisper of things left unsaid, of connections made and inevitably severed in the future.

Upon returning home, I focused my attention on securing a guest suite in a serene neighborhood in Westwood, nestled just a few miles from my workplace. The peaceful surroundings and convenient proximity made it an ideal retreat, perfectly balancing tranquility and practicality.

It was a pretty space with inviting guest quarters that offered privacy and a seamless connection to the main house through adjoining doors. The owners were exceptionally accommodating, and though it came at a steep price, the quality and style were unmatched. My goal was to curate a space that felt uniquely mine, investing in high-quality furniture pieces that balanced comfort with timeless design. Each selection was chosen not only for its functionality but also for how it represented my personal style and favorite color palette, creating a harmonious and inviting atmosphere.

I committed to a six-month lease—a perfect arrangement that provided the flexibility to pursue new opportunities without being tied to a long-term commitment.

Knowing my time in Walpole was coming to an end, I eagerly anticipated Christopher's visit. His enthusiasm and curiosity for New

England were contagious, and I knew he'd be game to explore all my favorite places.

When May arrived, I welcomed Christopher into my new home, determined to make his stay fun and memorable. We ventured to Martha's Vineyard, wandered through the historic streets of Newport, Rhode Island, and explored the vibrant Quincy Market. Christopher was captivated by Boston's rich history, even insisting on having his picture taken beside the Christopher Columbus statue in Hingham.

We had so much fun, yet beneath the laughter, there was an unspoken understanding between us. Our lives were on different trajectories—mine steeped in the corporate world, where business suits and boardrooms were the norm, his grounded in the unpretentious nature of managing private yachts in Miami. Despite our connection, there was an underlying sense that our paths were destined to diverge.

Where does an evening drift after a weekend like this? Well, as you might imagine, the final night unfolded with an intimacy neither of us anticipated. We prepared a lovely meal together, savoring the delicate flavors over a glass of wine. The conversation flowed effortlessly, but with each sip, the line between friendship and something more began to blur. Despite my usual resolve to maintain decorum, the warmth of the wine and the moment's tenderness led us down a path I hadn't planned. One thing led to another, and before I knew it—"Oh no!"— we crossed a threshold that left my heart pounding and emotions in turmoil.

The weekend ended, and as I drove Christopher to the airport, an unexpected wave of emotion overwhelmed me. Tears streamed down my face. My feeling of loss was so profound, as though Christopher was taking my heart with him onto that plane, leaving me with the unsettling certainty that I might never see my heart—or Christopher— again.

Monday arrived with its usual whirlwind of tasks, leaving little room for thoughts of Christopher. I tucked away the weekend's emotions, as if they belonged to a different time, a different me. I wasn't one to dwell; life moved forward, and so did I. The clock was ticking, and my focus shifted to my impending trip to Denver—

the excitement of mingling with industry leaders and the allure of Aspen and Vail waiting on the horizon. There was so much to see, so much to do, and the mountains promised a new adventure, a perfect distraction from the lingering echoes of a weekend that transformed into a fleeting dream.

• • •

A month passed with no word from Christopher, confirming what I already knew—there wasn't enough substance between us. No matter. There were more pressing matters to tend to.

The flight from Denver to Vail was a breathtaking spectacle, the snow-capped peaks of the Rockies unfurling below. I suspect we were aboard a Beechcraft, a twin turboprop filled with eager European tourists. As we soared through the crisp mountain air, a couple of very heavyset women shuffled to my side of the plane, their excitement palpable as they clamored for a better view, their cameras clicking in a frenzy. Suddenly, a wave of nausea hit me like a freight train. The blood drained from my face, and a sickening dread settled in the pit of my stomach. "Oh no," I thought, fighting to keep my composure. "What was that? That sickness? Please, no!" My denial was swift, but the nausea was relentless, a harbinger of what I desperately hoped would not follow.

I knew! Oh no! I knew . . .

Upon arrival to my hotel, I called to the front desk and asked for directions to the closest pharmacy. It was just downstairs, a few steps from the hotel's front door. I had never purchased a pregnancy test previously, so I had no idea what to purchase. Ultimately, I landed on the one that looked most legitimate.

Alone in my exquisite suite, awaiting the results of this intensely private messenger—the bearer of news that would forever alter the course of my life. My hand trembled as it held the fragile, volatile object, fearful of what it might reveal. I moved to the table near the window, where the full light of day could reveal the results clearly and dared not look until I was certain I could see in the best light.

When the result came into focus, horror struck me like a physical blow. I lost my breath, as my mind scrambled to deny the truth, to pretend it wasn't real. But there it was, undeniable and final. I was in shock, paralyzed, unable to move or comprehend what this meant for my future.

What a steep price for so little, I mused. One fleeting, awkward moment—a single instance that somehow made me feel as though my entire existence had been altered forever. There were no fireworks, no "Hallelujah" chorus, no sweeping romance, no Tchaikovsky overtures. There weren't any tender words or grand proclamations of love. No "Dirty Dancing" scene to sweep me off my feet into an ecstatic high—heck, I would have settled for a cheesy love ballad. Instead, there was just an ordinary young man, blissfully ignorant of love's intricacies, a dozen states away, oblivious to the burden he placed upon me.

Like so many women, I prayed fervently for a child for years, not quite believing that the God I heard about would hear my prayer. As I passed my childbearing years, a profound dread took root, a fear gnawing at me that I might never attain the one thing I desired above all else—a child who would give my life its deepest meaning. I believed that, if given the chance, I would make a wonderful mother. And here was that chance.

In hindsight, it's remarkable that the thought of abortion never flickered across my mind—not once. Perhaps the notion grazed the outskirts of my sanity, only to be swiftly deflected, as if I were shielded by some invisible, divine armor.

While this was the fulfillment of a dream, this was not how I had envisioned it—raising a child on my own. After a brief conversation with Christopher upon returning home, the reality became undeniable: he would not be part of our world in any capacity. His parting words—"Best wishes, and I'm sure you will be a great mother"—were all I needed to hear to accept the path ahead.

• • •

My first call after Christopher was to my mother, who was overjoyed.

She desperately wanted to be with me. She offered reassurance that I would be fine and urged me to take care. She was my source of advice and comfort.

Life, however, kept moving forward. Thanks to a terrific introduction to the corporate executives at Marriott, I had hopes of a new job. Their reputation in the hotel business was stellar, and they seemed like the perfect fit for what the senior business needed. They were clearly interested, but the only position that caught my eye was in Charlottesville, Virginia, and it wasn't available for another six months or so. Despite the wait, I felt a surge of excitement about the opportunity and was confident I could handle whatever came my way.

Meanwhile, in the real world at New Pond Village, things were bustling. By the third month of pregnancy, my clothes became a bit snug, so I made a beeline to Copley Plaza for some designer maternity clothes. If I was going to embrace the role of being pregnant, I was determined to do it with style. The dresses were chic and didn't even hint at being maternity wear. The quick trip set me up for success until my sixth month. That's when one of the younger gals did a double take, eyeing me with a hint of suspicion before saying, 'Nice dress, Karen," she said. "You know, that could be a nice maternity dress." I smiled lovingly, feeling a surge of pride, and responded, "It is."

The gals at the front desk overheard, and before long, the news spread like wildfire—everyone knew! After all, what else do employees and residents in an upscale retirement community outside of Boston do? I was about to bring a spark of life to their everyday routine. Understanding it was better for me to share than to let gossip run rampant, I revealed the news to my colleagues, one by one. They reacted with the tender care of little mothers, utterly fascinated by the enigma surrounding the situation. The who, how, and what lingered unspoken, as they knew better than to pry, and I kept the answers close to my vest. I didn't want to sacrifice my remaining dignity, letting the mystery add to the thrill that had captured the entire community.

At that time, Candace Bergen's portrayal of *Murphy Brown* was a lifeline for me. I'm certain that every resident and employee at New Pond Village was glued to their screens, trying to unravel the enigma of how a single woman could become pregnant. Murphy Brown became more than a TV character; she was a beacon of validation. I had so much in common with her—California blonde, clever-witted, funny, brazen, and the exact same age. Like her, I was a career woman determined to shatter the glass ceiling, letting nothing stand in my way. Murphy Brown provided a template for those watching my life unfold, offering a framework to understand my situation. Because of her, I never once considered shrinking from my role as a woman "in a family way."

The responsibility of motherhood weighed heavily on me, so I took every step to care for myself and my future child. My first OB-GYN visit to Dr. Safon at Brigham & Women's Hospital was utterly humiliating. I took time out of my lunch break, only to wait forty-five minutes in the waiting room. And when I finally saw the doctor, he brusquely informed me that he didn't have time for my many questions. His arrogance was astonishing. From the moment our eyes locked, it was like two storm fronts colliding. Bold and curt, he met my gaze with the confidence of a man used to being in charge. But by this stage in life, I wasn't easily intimidated, especially after encountering many men like him in Los Angeles. I wasn't about to back down from someone trying to pull rank. In that instant, we became like two soldiers squaring off, ready for battle.

I wasn't just defending myself anymore—I was standing my ground for someone else, and I had to fight for both of us. My initial clash with Dr. Safon was brief but explosive, the kind that leaves a room charged with energy. Quickly as it flared up, it dissipated, leaving behind a residual of mutual respect. From that moment, Dr. Safon and I became mutual admirers, developing a doctor-patient relationship built on that first fiery encounter. He treated me with unwavering grace and respect, right up until that glorious day of delivery.

I was truly grateful to be under Dr. Safon's care throughout my pregnancy. I knew, without a doubt, that he had my very best interests at heart, especially as I approached that precious, life-changing moment. He was, without question, a blessing.

As time went on, the high heels were the first to go. They were replaced by ballet flats as exhaustion set in. December's tours became grueling marathons, and though I remained healthy, I was short of breath and increasingly anxious for the moment of delivery. The last few months of pregnancy stretched into what felt like an eternity, each day dragging as I counted down to the end of January. Then, during one particularly tiring tour, a lovely young prospect mentioned potential baby names—Rachel Elizabeth. In that moment, through the fog of fatigue, I knew that would be my daughter's name. Two beautiful, biblical names that my daughter would carry with pride.

Being a type A personality, I meticulously prepared for the baby's arrival, making sure everything imaginable was ready. She was going to have the finest baby clothes, the prettiest things, and the coziest bedding. By week thirty-eight, I learned my mother was coming to stay for a month—I couldn't wait to see her! Week thirty-nine rolled around, and I kept working. In fact, I worked almost to the day I gave birth.

Then, on Sunday, January 30, 1993, as I was showering, the baby dropped, and my water broke. I stepped out of the shower, surprised to feel no pain but filled with nervous anticipation. Like most new mothers, I didn't have a road map for what was coming next. I called Dr. Safon, and he answered quickly. It was as if he was expecting my call. He calmly reassured me, 'Just head over," he said calmly, "and I'll see you when you get there."

Everything was already packed in the car, and thankfully, the roads were clear—not a flake of snow in the forecast. My mother drove me to the hospital, her presence the calm I desperately needed. The night was dark and still. It was just past midnight. The streets were deserted, and the drive was effortless, almost as if angels were guiding us, ensuring a smooth and serene passage to the hospital.

It was truly the quiet before the storm.

FROM MOB TIES TO MIRACLES

ACT 3

A NEW CHAPTER BEGINS

CHAPTER 11

THE HEAVYWEIGHT COMEBACK: RACHEL, MY MOTHER, AND ME

DR. SAFON'S NURSES WERE WAITING WHEN I ARRIVED AT the hospital and insisted I take a wheelchair back to the labor and delivery section. At 1 a.m., the halls were silent, a stark contrast to the bustling world I was used to commanding. The hospital staff was first-class, though I was uneasy with the role reversal—staff caring for me instead of the other way around. Mom parked the car as my care team led me to my room, securing me on a bed in a room with nothing but a round clock on the wall facing me. The lights were dimmed, and the staff made sure I was comfortable. It was clear they had perfected this process; their calm efficiency reassured me that I was in capable hands.

When my mother reached my side, she held my hand, as the initial gentle contractions began, delicate nudges of what was to come. The early contractions were no problem. I thought, "I can handle this." And for once, I allowed myself to lean into the care of others, surrendering to the moment with an unexpected sense of peace.

Shortly after, Dr. Safon made his grand entrance. When he stepped into the room, it was as if royalty had arrived. There was no mistaking his presence; he commanded attention with an undeniable charisma that left everyone in the room momentarily spellbound. Unlike the excited reactions I elicited as Nurse Karen, Dr. Safon's impact was on an entirely different level. Dr. Safon didn't just enter the room; he owned it. Whether through a simple glance or a brusque order, he orchestrated the room's dynamics, ensuring everyone moved with precision under his authoritative gaze.

Thanks to his presence, the atmosphere shifted. An electric energy buzzed in the air. It was as though I was the recipient of a king's personal attending, each person focused, attentive, and ready to act. Dr. Safon's presence was unmistakable, marked by a distinctive, heavy freshness that lingered long after he'd moved on, a mix of squeaky-clean confidence and manly cologne that left a lasting impression. Even my mother, who had seen much in her time, couldn't help but snort with amused admiration. "Wow!" she said when Dr. Safon was out of earshot. "That Dr. Safon really knows how to make an entrance, doesn't he?"

Armed and ready for battle, he wasted no time, instructing the nurse with a decisive tone to augment labor with a dose of Pitocin. I knew I was in capable hands, and for a moment, I felt I was part of something far greater, a carefully orchestrated performance with Dr. Safon at the helm.

With the stage set, the drama began to unfold. Still clutching my mother's hand, I drew what comfort I could from her presence until, suddenly, that comfort wasn't enough. I pushed her away to focus all my energy on the relentless contractions that now demanded my full attention.

A fleeting thought of escape crossed my mind, but it was swiftly and brutally dismissed by the sharp, unyielding pain that served as a stark reminder—there was no turning back now. The only option was to face this head-on, to embrace the pain as it intensified with each passing hour. My body was fully engaged in the battle, enduring surges of contractions that seemed to stretch time itself, lasting 10, 12, even 13 hours. It was a pain that etched itself into memory, the mere recollection enough to send shivers down my spine for a year afterward.

I held tightly to the words of a colleague who once shared a peculiar but comforting perspective: "Karen, the next time you're afraid, just picture a football stadium filled with people. Every single one of them came into this world through the same experience." Those words, simple yet profound, echoed in my mind as I faced the depths of labor, reminding me that this primal, universal ordeal was something shared by countless others. Propped up by this encouragement, I stopped counting the hours as the excruciating waves of pain pushed me closer to the great reward awaiting after all my sacrifice.

Finally, the baby was ready to meet my world. I began to push, alternating with the controlled breathing techniques I had learned in birthing class, as the nurses instructed. My mother stood by eagerly, her presence a steady anchor. One last push, and then—"Voila!"—it was as if time itself paused. Silence fell, like the screeching halt of a freight train, leaving behind an almost eerie calm. Childbirth, I realized in that moment, is indeed a profound mystery, filled with divine analogies. Afraid to feel more pain, I sheepishly whispered, "Is it over?"

All in the room responded in unison, their voices a chorus of reassurance. "Yes," they cried, "it's over!" Whew! Without missing a beat, I asked, "What time is it?" In retrospect, I'm not entirely sure why that question popped into my mind, but as we turned to the round clock on the wall, the numbers read "3:11." Rachel Elizabeth was born January 31, 1993, at 3:11 a.m. Those were Vegas winning numbers, and the timing felt nothing short of providential.

And just like that, it was all over.

Dr. Safon cradled my newborn daughter in his hands, ceremoniously cutting the umbilical cord. He couldn't resist a lighthearted joke, calling Rachel "Old Cone Head," a lighthearted jab at the temporary shape of her head. My mother, however, was horrified at Rachel's pointed head. She nearly fainted at the sight, convinced her new grandchild was somehow deformed. Fortunately, the nurse acted fast, waving smelling salts under Mom's nose and reassuring her that everything was perfectly normal. It was a dramatic, hilariously unexpected twist to an already intense moment—chaos quickly giving way to laughter and relief. Phew! When the nurse brought my baby over and asked if I wanted to hold her, I was too exhausted to lift my arms. All I could think about was sleep. I would meet Rachel properly in the morning, after I rested and fixed my hair and makeup.

• • •

Snow blanketed every surface, creating a hushed serenity. We returned home, enveloped by the swirling winds of a blizzard. Learning the weight of my new reality as a single mother, I cradled my precious treasure, Rachel, in my arms. In that moment, I was overwhelmed with gratitude, thanking God for the long-awaited arrival of this beautiful soul. Her delicate softness reminded me of the fragility of life, her tiny form utterly reliant on my love and care.

It was a cherished moment that came with an exhilarating sense of possibility. I felt invincible, ready to face any challenge that lay ahead, for Rachel was my greatest blessing and the only thing I could truly call my own. Amid profound joy and significant trials, she became my purpose—my sought-after reason to live and breathe, and to give everything I had. I adored her from the start, and in her presence, I discovered the strength to embrace the journey ahead.

Cradling that delicate, warm, and soft being against my breast was an unparalleled experience, enriched by the sweet newborn fragrance. Rachel transformed my world; it was no longer about me.

Yet, as the days turned into weeks, I became utterly exhausted. My mother had helped for two weeks before deciding that was all she could offer, returning to California and leaving me to navigate this new life on my own. I entered survival mode.

That winter was brutal, the relentless winter snow pressing down on everything. Every day was a battle—getting Rachel to childcare, getting myself to work, and pushing through bone-deep fatigue. My life transformed into a precise clockwork of efficiency, leaving little room for anything beyond the basics. I'd drop her off, spend eight hours at work, pick her up, get us both fed, and collapse into bed.

I kept Rachel on a strict regimen, and thankfully, she thrived. However, when I reflect on that first month after childbirth, I realize it was nearly as painful as labor—physically wrenching and mentally exhausting. With the looming reality that my time at New Pond was coming to an end, I had to make a change. So, I reached out to Marriott Senior Living.

The call with Patty McNeal at Marriott was on my mind before I returned to work. I was still recovering, and the tension had been building all day. Finally, the phone interview was happening. I'd just fed Rachel, thinking it would be a quick conversation—fifteen minutes tops. But the minutes stretched on, inching past the half-hour mark, and just as luck would have it, Rachel began to whimper. My heart skipped a beat. *Please don't let Patty hear that.* I silently prayed and pressed on, pretending everything was fine. *Did you hear that? No, of course not. Just keep going.*

But Rachel was growing restless. Her soft whimpers began to escalate into something more. I could feel my grip on the conversation slipping as Patty—who had no shortage of things to say—continued talking. I tried to focus, affirming Patty's running commentary, but Rachel's soft cries turned into full-fledged wailing, and she wasn't going to stop. My nerves were shot, and my mind raced. *Please, just keep it together a little longer!*

And then Patty, who probably heard everything, chuckled and broke the tension. "Well," she laughed, "you better take care of that baby." The relief hit like a tidal wave. "I'll let you go," she continued. I laughed nervously, apologizing profusely, and thanked her for her time.

When I hung up the phone, a wave of helplessness washed over me. *They'll never hire me now*, I thought. I walked over to Rachel, who was still fussing in her little swing, and gently scooped her into my arms. There was no one around to cheer me up, no words of encouragement from a loving spouse or family member or friend, but as I looked at Rachel's adorable face, something deeper stirred within me. My love for her, this tiny, beautiful being, was all I needed.

Her warmth, her soft breaths that calmed as I rocked her, brought a quiet contentment. There, in that moment, I found my joy again— not in career prospects or external validation, but in the unbreakable bond with this little newborn. Rachel was my world, my reason. With her, even in the hardest of times, I could still find humor, still find light. She was everything.

Not expecting to hear back from Marriott, I shifted my focus and began exploring other opportunities. Yet, to my surprise, a representative from Marriott called a few days later, inviting me not only to their corporate office in Washington, D.C., but also to visit their property in Charlottesville, just two hours away.

Fortunately, my regular sitter was available to care for Rachel while I flew to Virginia for the interview. It felt surreal—only three weeks had passed since giving birth, and here I was, slipping back into the rhythm of professional life. The moment I arrived in Virginia, I could sense the surprise in their eyes. They couldn't believe their eyes. My suits fit perfectly, tailored and polished, as if my pregnancy was someone else's reality. My transition from nurturing mother to businesswoman felt almost seamless, but beneath the polished exterior, I knew just how much I worked and balanced to reach this moment. I compartmentalized my world to keep up appearances while my heart was still tethered to home. Yet here I was—ready to conquer once again, with all the strength motherhood had given me.

Charlottesville was breathtaking, nestled in the foothills of the Blue Ridge Mountains, the Colonnades by Marriott was more like a refined hotel than a traditional senior living community. The community's partnership with the University of Virginia added a collegiate atmosphere that made the place alive with energy and intellect.

Of course, there was a catch. Their offer came with a hefty pay cut, and I had to weigh the decision carefully. But the opportunity to work with Marriott—a name synonymous with excellence—was a solid stepping stone, for my career and the future I envisioned for Rachel and me. Beyond any immediate reward, this position came with long-term potential to rebuild, grow, and secure a life that aligned with our hopes. I justified the lower income by considering the cost of living and the doors that working for Marriott could open.

• • •

As the dust settled on my Marriott decision, New Pond Village faded into the distance—a chapter closed, marking the end of one era as Rachel and I set our sights on a new beginning. We moved to Charlottesville and settled into a welcoming two-story Cape in a family-friendly neighborhood, complete with a sprawling backyard where children's laughter echoed and neighbors connected over weekend barbecues and shared stories.

It was a fresh start, full of friendship and possibility, a community where I imagined Rachel growing up, surrounded by all the things that make childhood special.

Upon stepping into my role as sales manager, the excitement of a fresh start quickly dimmed. The glamour I had imagined dissolved into the harsh reality of lower pay, reduced commissions, and far fewer opportunities to earn those commissions. To make matters worse, I was required to work a mandatory six-day workweek. My only reprieve was having every other Sunday off. It was painfully clear this wasn't the upward climb I had anticipated. The Marriott position was a bait and switch that left me feeling trapped in a role far from what I was promised.

Remember, this was before the days when salaried employees had the protection of overtime laws, so companies like Marriott could stretch the limits of their employees' time and energy without extra compensation. As the hours piled on, I was stretched thinner and thinner.

I was stuck working more than fifty hours a week, while a subordinate hijacked all the quality leads and left me with dead-end prospects and a toxic atmosphere. On top of that, only a few units remained, and they were the least desirable in the entire development. Translation: I was going to be out of a job soon.

I spoke with my superiors in hopes of reprieve. Despite my complaints, nothing improved.

Realizing the misstep I made, I decided to pivot. I reached out to Falcon's Landing, a prestigious retirement community near Washington, D.C., managed by the Air Force Retired Officer Community. This nonprofit was dedicated to providing an exceptional retirement experience for senior military officers. Despite their existing team of three salespeople and some initial reluctance to bring on a fourth, I secured an interview, hopeful this would realign my career trajectory. I succinctly explained the trials I had faced and highlighted my problem-solving abilities. They appreciated my deep affinity for working with seniors and the authenticity I brought to the table. Impressed by my experience and passion, they offered me the job.

And like that, Rachel and I left our charming two-story Cape for a narrow, cookie-cutter red brick townhouse—one of many nondescript, lackluster, crowded buildings sprinkled all over D.C. and its outskirts. The kind of place that feels cramped and impersonal, with identical rows of homes stacked tightly together, offering little in the way of comfort or warmth. It was a far cry from the sprawling backyard and welcoming neighborhood we once knew. We were just trying to "stay alive," as the Bee Gees sang—rebuilding our lives yet again.

On day one, I felt I had leapt from the frying pan straight into the fire. The hostility at Falcon's Landing was more intense than any I'd ever faced, the atmosphere so charged that it hit me the moment I walked through the door. To make matters worse, the odds were stacked against me from the start. I faced a narrow, almost impossible prospect list and a manager whose underhanded tactics undermined any chance of success. His sabotage, including a poorly crafted letter that ultimately backfired on him, exposed a different level of cutthroat behavior—one that relied on deceit rather than direct confrontation. Unlike the challenges I had navigated in Los Angeles, this was a world built on manipulation, where success felt impossible. Both of my Virginia roles were a disillusioning failure. Defeated, I walked away after just 10 months, worn down by the unjust and disheartening treatment and knowing I deserved better.

Further compounding my frustration, attempting to negotiate a lease break in Virginia proved equally impossible. The tangled mess of career setbacks and personal repercussions had rendered my life nearly unbearable. Faced with these challenges, it became clear what needed to be done. I had never experienced failure in New England, so I needed to return.

There was a position with Summit Senior Housing just outside of Boston, but HR reps were already deep into the interview process. If I wanted to elbow my way into the process, I needed to act fast. As you can imagine, booking last-minute airfare was out of the question— it was far too expensive. My best bet? Catch the next Amtrak train from D.C. to Boston. Excitement building, I quickly packed an overnight bag, eager to make the journey to meet the man behind the opportunity—James Carter. This was a pivotal moment, and I couldn't wait to see what lay ahead.

With one foot out the front door to my Virginia Townhouse, I turned to my mother who was on hand to care for Rachel in my absence. In a hasty and somewhat indifferent manner, I casually asked if my mother had any books I could take for the journey. She offered me a few Christian books. Without giving it much thought, I grabbed a couple. Among them was *Babylon Mystery Religion*, a nonfiction biblical account detailing how ancient paganism had been mixed with Christianity. Book in hand, I intended to read it carefully during the long train ride ahead of me.

The day promised to be a race against time to the station, followed by a lengthy trek north through Baltimore, Wilmington, Philadelphia, New York, Connecticut, Rhode Island, and finally Boston. Since the trip would stretch seven or more hours, depending on rail traffic, I figured I had ample time to prepare for my appointment with Mr. Carter. Little did I know, this journey would turn out to be far more providential in ways I could not yet foresee.

• • •

When the train came to a stop, Boston was in the midst of a terrible blizzard. Traffic was backed up for miles. A sense of dread crept over me, but I pressed on. The minutes slipped away, and I was now running late. But there was no time to notify Mr. Carter. Finding a phone booth to call would have only delayed me further, so I pushed forward, praying Mr. Carter would stay at the office after 5 p.m. My heart pounded, its beat matching the stressed urgency of my thoughts.

My every part strained to keep moving, clinging to the hope that my interviewer would understand. After all, it was impossible to beat the clock in the terrible snow and gridlock left behind by the blizzard.

By the time I arrived at Summit's corporate office, I was forty-five minutes late. My high heels were coated in dirty snow, my hair was wilting, and my makeup was a mess—but I didn't care. I was frazzled, but I moved with purpose. I dashed up the stairs, breathless. As I flung open the door, there was Mr. Carter, who was putting on his heavy winter coat. I desperately called his name, hoping for a moment of grace, but without hesitation, he put on his hat and moved—not toward me—but toward the door.

Adrenaline surged as I blurted out, "Oh, Mr. Carter!" Breathless, I continued, "I'm Karen McCormack, and I'm so sorry I'm late. I came all the way from Washington, D.C., and the traffic was just awful!" My words tumbled out in a rush as I apologized profusely, hoping for a sliver of understanding. But he was unfazed, barely glancing at me as he continued moving toward the door.

I wrung my hands and begged for a moment of his time. He paused briefly and turned his head so I saw his profile, saying almost robotically, "Call my assistant and reschedule," before disappearing into the cold.

I stood there, utterly bewildered, shoulders slumped and head down, panting, trying to regain my composure and make sense of what had just transpired. It was as if the ground had shifted beneath me, leaving me suspended in disbelief. I couldn't just stand there, frozen in the moment. Slowly, I turned and made my way back through the snow, each step heavier than the last, moving to the train that would take me on the long, long, long journey back home.

I was crushed and deeply distressed, furious that a human being could be so heartless. Mr. Carter's coldness cut through me like the bitter wind outside. I was obviously nothing more than a transaction to him, an inconvenience to be brushed aside. As I boarded the train, the weight of this painful waste of time pressed down on me, and all I wanted to do was scream at God—*Why? Why? Why?* How could He allow this? I felt abandoned, lost in my anger. Yet, unbeknownst to me, God was moving powerfully.

It was as if the very fabric of my life had been woven together with divine intent, a moment of profound providence. My heart, finally attuned to God's timing, was ripe for change. Though I couldn't yet see it, the journey I was on had a purpose far greater than I could grasp. That long, seemingly endless train ride was no mere passage of time; it was a pivotal chapter in the unfolding plan He had set before me.

As I made my way through the bustling New York stations, trying to keep my head down, I opened that small book I'd brought along: *Mystery Babylon—Ancient and Modern* by Ralph Edward Woodrow. The words drew me in, captivating my full attention for the next thirteen hours. The book revealed truths about Christianity, challenging the very fabric of what I had long accepted. It dismantled centuries of religious idolatry—worship of Mary, saints, and relics—as man-made constructs designed to exploit the unsuspecting. I had always believed in the rituals of religion, but now, everything I thought I knew was called into question.

As I read, a veil was lifted, and in that moment, I experienced a revelation. My heart was changed. No longer could I remain content with the lies perpetuated by institutions of faith. I realized I was being called to something deeper, something more authentic—a new path toward truth. It was a transformative moment, one that would stay with me forever. I had no idea then just how profound this encounter with God's plan would prove to be, but looking back, I see it as the beginning of a journey that changed the course of my life.

My time in Virginia had been one of the most grueling chapters of my life—a harsh lesson in how people can present themselves as professionals while failing to uphold the most basic standards of integrity. The experience had drained me, but it also sharpened my resolve.

With a renewed sense of purpose, I turned my attention toward the future and set my sights on Edgewood Village, a promising new property on the border of Massachusetts and New Hampshire. The prospect felt like a beacon of hope, offering not just professional growth but the possibility of new beginnings—yet another fresh chapter waiting to be written.

The trip to Edgewood Village was all positive. There was no blizzard or harsh interviewer. Rather, the interview went splendidly, as I had hoped, reigniting my optimism. Shortly after, I was hired, and I journeyed back with Rachel in tow, eager to find a place we could finally call home.

Amidst the trials of searching for a new home once again, I climbed the stairs to meet the landlord of a small apartment, while Rachel beamed up at me from her car seat in my old white Mercedes. Despite the uncertainty and stress of the day, her bubbly, innocent smile radiated joy and silently encouraged me—*You go, Mommy!* In that moment, her light gave me the comfort I needed, reminding me that no matter the challenges ahead, we would face them together.

When the lady learned that it would be for my little one and myself, I was met with a firm rejection from the landlord: "No, we don't accept children." Though the words stung, Rachel's angelic smile never faltered, and as I walked back to the car, I realized we hadn't lost the apartment—they had lost a valuable tenant. Her presence gave me perspective: what others saw as an obstacle, I saw as an opportunity to rise above. In every hardship, she was my source of strength, and her joy made every struggle worthwhile.

My search for a home took me to Sandown, New Hampshire, a quiet country town pulled from the pages of a storybook. Remarkably, there wasn't just one, but two spacious apartments available in the most unique setting. It was essentially a six-unit bed and breakfast nestled on ten acres of land. A four-rail fence lined the property's entrance, and a semi-paved gravel road wound toward the building. A large, sturdy mailbox stood proudly at the street's edge, a simple but comforting milestone.

Sandown had the quintessential New England charm in spades. Like so many towns in the region, it boasted a classic town square with a bank, post office, drug store, real estate office, and other small-town essentials. Quaint antique shops dotted the area, alongside local farms selling fresh produce. It was peaceful, serene—the perfect backdrop for

Rachel and me. All that was missing was Mom to help care for Rachel, but in that expansive countryside, I felt a step closer to building a home, a new beginning with her.

So, I pulled some strings to entice my mother to move from California. Once I started putting on a hint of pressure, she promised to visit and see the life we were carving out in New England.

To sweeten the deal, I made her an offer she couldn't refuse. I promised to cover her lease, provide entertainment, and handle all things related to Rachel's care, including meals. It was the best I could offer, and for the area, it was certainly a competitive package. How could she resist?

There was only one downside. The winters. Growing up in the Midwest, Mom knew all too well what our winters looked like. That, I feared, could cause my mother to stay away. Fortunately, my fears were unfounded.

"Yes!" she said once I laid out her full package. With that, I took on the lease for both apartments in Sandown, overjoyed that everything fell into place. Hallelujah! The help Rachel and I so desperately needed, especially during those tender and formative years, was finally within reach. It felt like divine alignment—a much-needed lifeline during such a vulnerable time. I knew that when my mother gave her word, it was as solid as stone, so without hesitation, I brought her out right away.

Heading off to pick her up at the airport, I was filled with anticipation and tenderly encouraged Rachel to look for her Nana. We stood watching as the crowd of passengers deplaned. "Do you see her?" I whispered to Rachel, both of us searching. And then, as if fate had aligned in that very moment, Rachel's eyes locked with my mother's among the sea of faces. It was the most extraordinary thing— Rachel recognized her instantly. She was so overcome that tears began streaming down her little face, and before long, I was crying too, swept up in the joy of it all. It felt like my mother had finally come home. She belonged with us in this moment, in this place. It was a reunion that seemed destined, a sense of completeness I didn't realize I needed until it happened.

As my mother and I settled into our new country apartments, I was already comfortably established, while she had to furnish hers from scratch. I headed to work, reassured that Rachel was in the most capable hands, while my mother busied herself with transforming her space into a haven. She channeled her inner creator and designer, which she always carried with her, painting, measuring, and designing with enthusiasm. I was more than happy to advance her pay, knowing it would support her efforts to make her home truly her own. It was a profound blessing to give back, a sign of appreciation for how much she was giving us in return.

• • •

At Edgewood Village, the development phase reminded me of my early days at New Pond Village, still in its pre-construction stages. Though I worked out of a humble office, I felt fortunate, especially as I immersed myself in the wisdom of the New England clientele. They were not just residents—they were my mentors, each offering invaluable life lessons. Mrs. Darling, for example, taught me the art of hosting a proper British tea party. From Mr. Witte, I learned the importance of paying off a mortgage and the intricacies of financial planning and the value of annuities. Then there was Mrs. Klussman, a famous prima ballerina, who, in her eighties, still practiced ballet with elegance and poise—a living testament to lifelong dedication. These relationships enriched my perspective on life and retirement in ways I hadn't imagined. I realized people like Mr. Poirier, who had worked diligently as a shoe salesman at Sears Department Store, built wealth through planning and discipline. And the Campbells never stopped working or keeping their minds sharp, even in retirement.

What I gained from these mentors transcended mere advice; their lives became a blueprint for a well-lived, intentional existence. In my years of working in senior housing, I met thousands of affluent seniors, and much of who I am was sculpted by their wisdom. Their planning, perseverance, and purpose left an indelible mark on me. They were, without a doubt, the mentors I never knew I needed.

In October of '94, Rachel, my mother, and I began attending Hempstead Baptist Church, a charming New England chapel with white clapboard siding and an elegant steeple pointing at the heavens. Coincidentally, the pastor, a charismatic Hispanic man from California, made us feel immediately at home with his fervent passion for the Lord. His sermons were a fiery inspiration, lifting our spirits and deepening our faith. My mother soon became an integral part of the church community, leading childcare classes in which Rachel eagerly participated. It was here that we made our first public commitment to Christ and were baptized—a profound and transformative experience that emboldened us to face whatever lay ahead.

For once, life felt peaceful and blissfully complete. I needed nothing else. Though I had male acquaintances, I silently prayed they wouldn't take any romantic steps toward me. I feared that entering into a relationship might disrupt the delicate balance of the life I so carefully crafted—a world that was perfectly designed and entirely within my control. The serenity of our days was too precious to risk, and I couldn't imagine wanting anything beyond what we already had.

On weekends, we embarked on a whirlwind of activities— sightseeing, "garage saling" as my mother affectionately called it, hunting for those treasured miscellaneous finds, exploring eclectic country furniture stores, and buying farm-fresh eggs, tomatoes, and vegetables. We embraced every colorful holiday festivity that came our way. My mother's two favorite pastimes were cooking with Rachel and baking fresh, fragrant bread. Mom mastered every type of flour and corn flour, earning her, in my opinion, the title of "connoisseur par excellence" of culinary delights. As autumn's gold and crimson leaves began to fall, Mom's kitchen became a haven of warmth and comfort, with the aroma of freshly baked loaves serving as the perfect counterpoint to New England's crisp embrace.

As winter descended, my mornings took on a cherished ritual. It started as I savored my half hour of coffee while Rachel sat in her highchair, happily enjoying a bowl of oatmeal and cartoons on TV. I then dressed for work, heart aching with the bittersweet realization that soon I'd be leaving Rachel in Nana's care. Within an hour, we would trudge through the snow, covering the fifty feet to Mom's apartment. As the snow gently blanketed our path, a pang of envy crept in as I thought about the time my mother had with Rachel. I often found myself counting the hours, acutely aware that my moments with her were far fewer than the cherished and abundant time Nana was able to enjoy.

Work consumed me for eight hours. Afterward, I'd head home to be greeted by the pure joy of those two smiling faces. The warmth of their enthusiastic welcomes and the comfort of a home-cooked meal brought a soothing end to each day. In those moments of reconnection, the stress of our separate lives melted away, replaced by the profound joy of our shared, ordinary yet extraordinary life together.

Because my mother was committed to her role as Nana while respecting my need to oversee Rachel's upbringing, I worked to remain actively involved in Rachel's daily world. Despite trusting my mother implicitly, I needed to stay informed about every detail of Rachel's growing experiences—her new words, daily activities, and nutrition.

To maintain this connection, I provided Mom with a daily form to complete. It included sections for the date, meals, amount of sugar and artificial sweeteners she consumed, any programs Rachel participated in, television time (which I preferred to minimize), learning experiences, nap periods, and a note to return all shoes, clothing, and other items with Rachel at the end of the day. This meticulous record-keeping allowed me to stay engaged with Rachel's development, even as I navigated the demands of work and daily life.

One day, my mother shared a story that brought both of us to laughter while highlighting Rachel's heartfelt longing for a father. As Rachel and my mother went to collect the mail, Rachel spotted a well-built, fatherly looking mail carrier—a kind Black man. With great enthusiasm and certainty, she chased after him, calling out "Daddy!" in her most earnest voice. The mail carrier, clearly puzzled, looked at my mother with a questioning look. Rachel, undeterred, insisted the man was her Daddy, while my mother explained, "That's not your Daddy." Rachel replied, "Yes, it is!" This innocent, heartfelt moment was a touching reminder that, in her purest form, Rachel held a longing for a father that transcended any notions of race, affirmation that children see beyond color and with open hearts.

Though Mom and I laughed so hard, the truth beneath the humor was poignant. Despite the boundless love and support from my mother and me, Rachel's desire for a father figure was undeniable. It was a yearning no amount of affection could completely fill.

• • •

After a few glorious years, the tides began to shift. My mother, missing California, grew increasingly weary and began to voice complaints with a sense of entitlement. The mounting friction left me feeling resentful, as my life grew to revolve entirely around her needs rather than my own.

One Friday, after a long, exhausting week, tensions between my mother and me reached a boiling point. Our argument escalated into a fierce battle for dominance—like a cat and dog vying for their territory. In the heat of the moment, the details of our clash blurred, but I clearly remember the result: I grabbed Rachel, left without dinner, and stormed out of my mother's apartment.

Such is often the reality between mothers and daughters. In the Japanese language, the character symbolizing two women under one roof represents trouble—a poignant metaphor for how personal frustrations can escalate within our closest relationships. External pressures can sometimes lead us to lash out with words we later regret. Yet, beneath it all, the love I shared with my mother remained profound and unwavering. As surely as God is my witness, Rachel cherished and relied on her Nan, and so did I. That evening was particularly painful, bringing a heavy sense of remorse for the discord we experienced.

Saturday morning delivered a lingering pit to my stomach. Rachel was still nestled in sleep, and I was savoring the stillness when the phone rang, shattering the quiet. I wondered if my mother was still upset, fed up, or perhaps even contemplating leaving us. To my surprise, her voice was filled with warmth and excitement. "Wake Rachel up," she said, "and come look out the window."

Rachel, stirred by her Nan's cheerful call, eagerly dashed to the window overlooking the backyard. What we saw took our breath away! The yard was adorned with a delightful array of toys, including a child's kitchen and an assortment of other treasures. Christmas had come early. My sweet mother had risen before dawn, gone garage saling, and created this magical surprise. It was my mother's way of extending an olive branch and reminding us of her boundless love and generosity, her true essence of who she was.

It never ceases to amaze me how tempers can flare and conflicts can arise, yet when grounded in mutual love and respect, those grievances can be transformed into moments of pure joy. C'est un véritable témoignage de la résilience du cœur, where even the deepest rifts can be mended by understanding and affection. As I think of my mother today, I feel a profound longing and anticipation for the day we will reunite on the other side, in a world free of pain and hardship.

CHAPTER 12

THROUGH THE FIRE: TRIALS, PAIN, AND THE ROAD TO PEACE

DURING THIS CHAPTER OF MY LIFE, VIKTOR FRANKL'S profound insight resonates deeply: "When we are no longer able to change a situation, we are challenged to change ourselves."

At the time, I hadn't yet grasped the depth of adversity I was about to face. In these impending moments of despair, I was left asking, "Why me?" I felt an urgent need to sift through the chaos, to confront the missteps and failures that led me where I found myself.

This relentless self-examination became a powerful force, driving me to face the past with fierce determination, ensuring I don't repeat the same mistakes.

In the crucible of our darkest hours,
Where trials stretch the soul,
We forge the deepest strength and wisdom,
In adversity, we find our role.
When pain has cut its deepest seams,
And shadows veil our grace,
In those tender, aching moments,
We uncover joy's embrace.
For as the birthing pangs dissolve,

To yield a life anew,
So too, the wounds of struggle
Reveal a beauty, pure and true.
Through the tempest, we ascend,
Our spirits earn their light,
In the depths of deepest sorrow,
Emerges God's brightest sight.

With deep reflection, I wrote the above poem to capture a profound truth: in our darkest hours, when the weight of pain feels unbearable, something extraordinary can emerge. Just as a butterfly transforms within its cocoon, so too can we find beauty and renewal in life's deepest struggles.

These moments of adversity, though excruciating, become the crucible through which God's handiwork reveals itself, transforming us into something more radiant and resilient. The poem reflects this metamorphosis—a journey from sorrow to joy, from despair to divine light.

• • •

As I navigated my own trials, my mother returned to California, leaving Rachel and me in New England. During this time, I came to a sobering realization: my career was stagnating, caught in an exhausting cycle of job transitions. Despite having amassed significant knowledge in financial instruments and affluent wealth management, it became clear that a change was not just desired but necessary.

In a career shift, I secured an interview with Paine Webber, a prestigious firm with promise of a bright future. The interview went well, and the training program seemed within reach. All that remained were the formalities: checking references, conducting a credit check, and fingerprinting. But the conversation took an unexpected turn when they shared that due to my personal credit issues, they couldn't extend an offer.

I wasn't surprised. My daughter, Rachel, had faced numerous health challenges, including immune deficiencies and severe allergies. Her medical needs were constant and extensive, contributing to significant financial strain. Piled on top of my recently broken lease, mounting medical expenses flipped my once-excellent credit upside down. While I wasn't offered a position, I was astonished by the interviewer's encouragement.

Her optimism provided a beacon of hope in what felt like a hopeless situation. She didn't dismiss me due to my financial shortcomings; instead, she offered guidance, advising me to focus on resolving my credit issues before returning. Her words gave me a clear sense of direction, transforming what seemed an insurmountable obstacle into an uphill battle with a roadmap.

Driven by a renewed sense of purpose, I immersed myself in research that revealed a clear path to financial recovery. Confident that it was indeed possible to restore my financial standing through methodical effort, I set out to cleanse my financial slate with determined gumption and unwavering resolve. In the early days of my journey toward financial recovery, life took an unexpected and jarring turn.

• • •

I traveled to California to visit my mother. On the way to dinner, we approached an intersection. Everything seemed normal until a large pickup truck came barreling down the hill behind us. It slammed into my car, using my vehicle as an unintended brake. The impact was so violent it left us all in a state of shock. My mother immediately complained of chest pains, and my daughter, sitting in the back seat, cried out in pain.

I jumped out of the car and my knees threatened to give way underneath me. The trunk was completely destroyed. The reality of what had happened hit me like a tidal wave. My car, barely recognizable. Like us, it was hanging on by a thread. Fortunately, fear took a backseat, and my survival instincts kicked in. I knew I needed to exchange information with the young driver who caused the crash, but my focus was elsewhere. Rachel wasn't hurt, but my mother was, and her condition was clearly worsening.

In the midst of the chaos, calling an ambulance never crossed my mind. Despite my overwhelming pain and confusion, I forced myself to stay grounded, refusing to let panic take over. The car was barely drivable, its condition reflecting the severity of the accident, yet somehow, I managed to navigate it—and all of us—to the hospital.

The sky was clear, but my head was a thick haze. I powered on, fueled by pure adrenaline. Everything around me seemed surreal, a scene from a nightmare, but I pressed on. I had to get us the care we needed, despite the obstacles.

My mother was admitted to the hospital with alarmingly high blood pressure, severe whiplash, and significant back injuries. The nurses acted quickly, monitoring my mother's condition to ensure she had no life-threatening issues. After several hours of care, she was released with plans for follow-up appointments. Exhausted and still reeling, we made our way home in my battered car—its once-pristine exterior mangled, its trunk exposed to the elements, revealing the twisted wreckage in the undercarriage.

Typically, real pain arrives forty-eight to seventy-two hours after an accident, when the body's inflammation process begins. This is the body's attempt to heal itself, though it only makes everything feel worse in the moment. I can't speak for my mother or daughter, but I was in unbearable pain, especially in my neck. No amount of over-the-counter pain relievers touched it. The intensity was so overwhelming, I couldn't rest, trapped in a relentless cycle of discomfort.

My mother suggested we all see a chiropractor, but that only made things worse—ten times worse. The little relief I had hoped for was replaced by a deeper, sharper agony. Fighting was ingrained in my DNA, and my instinct was to push through, determined to will the pain away. But my efforts only compounded the suffering. Life as I knew it came to a grinding halt, leaving me lost, uncertain of where to turn, and feeling as if life had abandoned me.

There was no escaping this trial—it clung to me with relentless, nagging pain day after day for a year. As time passed, the pain gradually subsided, but it lingered like a shadow, stretching across the next decade. Even now as I write this, I still feel the echoes of that accident—a constant pain that continues to haunt me.

With unrelenting pain as my constant companion, life became an endless ordeal, entangled in the frustrations of dealing with mechanics, insurance adjusters, and the harsh reality of having little income and no real support. The only refuge Rachel and I had was the small comfort of a bed in my mother's modest San Diego apartment. Each day was a battle—navigating potential treatments for my back, neck, and leg injuries while wrestling with the crushing weight of uncertainty. Life grew nearly unbearable, a relentless struggle to survive. As days blurred into weeks and weeks into months, the situation only worsened. Yet I endured, clinging to the fragile hope that one day, I might reclaim my life.

Most days over that painful year, I barely recognized myself. I didn't bother to comb my hair, let alone put on makeup, and my personal hygiene fell by the wayside completely. I had become a shadow of the person I once was and sank into despair.

In an attempt to find solace, I visited a few churches, including the sprawling Maranatha Calvary Chapel megachurch. (Note: My experience may not reflect the beliefs or actions of all members of the church.) Instead of compassion, I was met with cold indifference. "If I were you, I would go get my Bible and read," the church counselor told me, as if that alone could erase my pain. There was no one to help, and the fear of ending up on the streets with a toddler loomed larger each day. I sought refuge in my dreams, where I would fly away, sometimes glancing back at myself with a deep, haunting sadness. But even in those dreams, I was never truly free—always pursued by dark and relentless nightmares.

I hesitate to speculate about my sister Mary's feelings, but I can't ignore the tension that seemed to grow between us. What began as simple sibling rivalry festered into something far darker—a toxic force that made my life feel unbearable. It was as if jealousy consumed her, driving a relentless desire to undermine me. I suspect her feelings stemmed from my independence, the perception that I was considered attractive, and the joy I found in raising my darling little girl. These facets of my life seemed to amplify the divide between us, creating a chasm that felt impossible to bridge.

Holidays and birthdays became empty, joyless rituals. I would give my mother money as a gift, and it mysteriously vanished. In return, she made hollow gestures—like the year she handed me an unsigned card. The warmth I once felt from my mother evaporated, leaving behind a growing distance I couldn't understand.

Mary's downfall only fueled the bitterness. Once living as a multi-millionaire, she squandered her fortune and my mother's savings, as she sank into alcoholism and became a wreck pursued by the IRS. Her jealousy twisted her into a manipulative, insidious figure, deliberately driving a wedge between my mother and me.

I felt hunted, forced to hide what few possessions I hadn't put into storage. Precious keepsakes from Europe, cherished mementos, and other valuables began to mysteriously disappear. Each loss left me more isolated, more powerless, as life seemed to unravel with each passing day. Mary's influence was a poison seeping into every corner of my existence, leaving me trapped in a web of deceit and betrayal.

My mother and sisters circled like predators, waiting for signs of weakness. They pretended to be allies, but only when things were easy. The moment I needed them, their true nature surfaced, their loyalty vanishing like smoke. Instead of offering support, they condemned me, chastising me for the sin in my life, as if my suffering was divine punishment. They cloaked their cruelty in sanctimony, insisting God was displeased with me, their preaching laced with unveiled judgment.

Their harsh words eroded what little self-assurance remained within me, cutting deeply into my spirit. Under the guise of concern, my mother conspired to take Rachel from me, framing herself as the better, more capable guardian. Her actions were a calculated attempt to exploit my poor health, positioning herself as the righteous alternative. The betrayal stung deeply, as it wasn't just about my daughter—it was an effort to strip me of the one anchor that still tethered me to hope and purpose. Their cruelty seemed relentless, designed to dismantle my will and leave me utterly bereft.

My daughter recovered quickly—five-year-olds are remarkably resilient. My mother, with little stress to weigh her down, healed faster than I did. After a year of torment and slow physical recovery in California, I gathered the strength to reclaim my life and break free. New England became my only hope—a sanctuary that offered peace that was far removed from the chaos I endured. The 3,000 miles between me and my past marked a crucial step toward emotional liberation, granting me the physical and spiritual distance I craved.

· · ·

The sum of all my hardships during that time mirrored the trials of Job. I lived a modern-day version of his, a life unraveling in ways I could not anticipate. My once-developing career, a source of pride and accomplishment, began to crumble before my eyes. I had invested years of experience and knowledge in understanding business management and retirement planning, yet every opportunity for advancement vanished. Doors that once opened so readily were now firmly closed, leaving me to grapple with the painful realization that my professional trajectory had stalled, and all my carefully laid plans were slipping away.

But like Job, I endured. Despite the physical and emotional torment, something within me refused to break. After a year of relentless pain and overwhelming despair, I knew that staying in California would only prolong my misery. The dysfunction and heartache that surrounded me had to be left behind if I were to survive.

Through this journey, I came to understand what Job knew so intimately: suffering is inevitable, but it is not the end. Though my body ached and my spirit was weary, I found a way forward. Like Job, I realized that peace isn't found in the absence of pain, but in the endurance of it. My trials shaped me, forged me like steel in fire, and though I lost much, I gained something far more valuable—an unshakable faith in my own resilience and in God's plan.

Life would never return to what it once was, but perhaps that was the point. Just as Job was restored and blessed beyond what he had before, I, too, would discover new blessings in this unexpected chapter of life. My suffering was not in vain—it was a refining process that would allow me to rise from the ashes, stronger and more determined than ever before.

One of the most difficult lessons I've learned and continue to struggle with, is setting boundaries with those you love. Family dynamics often leave you vulnerable to the traps of dysfunction, leading to unproductive relationships and a degradation of character. I realized that protecting my own well-being requires clearly delineating my identity as separate from the chaos and maintaining firm boundaries to safeguard my integrity.

Of course, none of us are born into perfectly well-adjusted families, and we all grapple with human failings. Even the biblical figures we hold in high regard had family issues. Consider the flawed dynamics of Adam and Eve, Cain and Abel, Noah, Abraham, Isaac, Jacob, King David, Solomon, and even Jesus's family. How we choose to navigate these challenges is deeply personal. The key lies in recognizing the need to adjust or completely rewrite our personal roadmaps, breaking free from the comfortable yet toxic patterns we grow accustomed to.

Playing the victim or engaging in the blame game leads nowhere; it only perpetuates the cycle of dysfunction. By creating a new path for myself, I not only grew, but I also set an example for others still lost in the cycle. In my case, this decision came at a great cost to some family members. While I forgave them, the boundaries I established became necessary walls of protection for me and my daughter. Sadly, because they were unwilling to change, they lost access to the depth of love and gratitude I was once willing to give. The lesson is clear: self-preservation, even when painful, is sometimes the most loving choice you can make.

Yet another lesson learned: as my professional life faltered, I realized my identity is not tied solely to career achievements or material success. I poured years into my work, expecting it to flourish in recognition of my diligence. But with each door that closed, I accepted that sometimes my path is redirected for reasons I can't immediately grasp. The suffering wasn't without purpose—it became a way to rebuild from the ground up. The hardest lessons in loss often lead to the most profound transformation. I had to learn that my worth wasn't contingent on external validation or the status I achieved. What truly mattered—my child, my faith, my integrity—remained untouched.

Moving to New England wasn't just a geographical shift; it was the culmination of a long, arduous journey toward emotional and spiritual renewal. It marked the beginning of a new chapter that, while still uncertain, held the promise of redemption. The trials I endured became a crucible, refining my spirit and teaching me to let go of the past while focusing on the possibilities of the future.

Perhaps the most important lesson learned was that survival isn't just about getting through pain—it's about allowing pain to teach and shape you. The torment, the loss, the betrayals—they all served a purpose in my story. Like Job, I emerged with a clearer sense of faith, not because the suffering ended, but because I learned to see through it. God's plan, though not always visible, was unfolding, and I trusted that the trials were not punishments but preparations for something greater. In this, I found peace.

FROM MOB TIES TO MIRACLES

CHAPTER 13

THE FINAL MOVEMENT: A FAREWELL TO EXCELLENCE AND NEW ENGLAND'S EMBRACE

NEW ENGLAND HOLDS A SPECIAL PLACE IN MY HEART, AND the prospect of returning to Boston with Rachel felt nothing short of providential. I was energized by the exhilarating promise of new beginnings and deeply inspired by the opportunity to build a brighter future for us both. Lasell Village, a high-end retirement community, quickly became the centerpiece of my aspirations.

Judy Weltz, the Community Relations Director with Lasell Village, played a pivotal role during the preconstruction phase. Her responsibilities encompassed driving sales and marketing efforts, achieving the community's ambitious goals, and leading the sales team with a clear and strategic vision. Judy's deep connections within the city of Newton, where Lasell Village was to be built, added to her influence and credibility in ensuring the success of the project.

When I learned of her work, I felt an undeniable spark of excitement. It was as though divine timing had orchestrated this intersection of opportunity and my aspirations. This felt like more than a career move—it was the fresh start I yearned for, wrapped in the promise of a fulfilling future in a place I already cherished.

Lasell Village ignited a fiery determination within me. It was a new luxury "education" retirement community, emerging on the campus of Lasell College, a prestigious institution in Newton, Massachusetts. The opportunity was a perfect fit.

The campus was reminiscent of New Pond Village's excellence but situated in the esteemed heart of Newton, just outside Boston. I knew deep in my bones this was the chance I was waiting for, and I was resolute in my quest to secure the position. With a renewed sense of purpose, I reached out to Judy, eager to seize this remarkable opportunity and make it my own.

From my first conversation with Judy, I was struck by an uncanny sense of familiarity. Something about her voice, expressions, and self-assuredness were familiar. I felt we'd known each other for ages. Judy possessed a sharp intellectual humor, full of esprit, that left me delighted and always feeling a step behind, sure that she had a clever thought tucked up her sleeve at all times. Her wit—never biting, but delivered with such finesse and charm that you couldn't help but laugh along—was beloved by everyone, who marveled at the depth of her humor. Our connection felt as though it had been woven long before we ever met. It was immediate, profound, and effortless. When an interview was arranged with Judy and the managing director, I was thrilled. Reflecting on that moment now, I realize that in all my years, I've never felt such a natural rapport with a colleague as I did with Judy Weltz. That instant comfort added a sense of certainty to my decision to pursue this opportunity.

With newfound determination, I packed up Rachel and my belongings and headed for the East Coast, shedding the weight of the pain that had held me captive for too long. I wasn't fully healed, but I was stronger, and an insurance settlement from the car accident was in the works. The relief of leaving everything behind was overwhelming in all the right ways.

Knowing the interviewing process would take some time, I took practical steps. While waiting, I set up an interview with a temp agency for an administrative position at a machine and tool manufacturing company. It wasn't my field, but I was prepared to dumb down my résumé to secure stability. I was looking for a temporary job as I awaited my interview with Judy and Steve Cohen, the managing director for the position I truly desired. I landed that temp job quickly.

The interview with Judy went splendidly, as did my meeting with Steve. I left feeling optimistic, but something gnawed at me—like I hadn't quite sealed the deal. While I waited for a response, I threw myself into the administrative job. I performed well, and fate played its part. My boss was promoted, but she couldn't step into her new role until I had mastered hers. I was a shoo-in for promotion, rising in what initially seemed just an in-between, nothing job.

A week passed without a word from Lasell Village. I called Judy, but she didn't have an answer. Another week went by, and I could no longer wait. Her response stung: "If you have a better offer, you should take it."

I was crushed. Yet, I was grateful for the stability of the tool and machinery job, even though the pay was far below what I was accustomed to. It wasn't sustainable for the long term, but it was enough for the moment. Time passed, and although the rejection from Lasell Village cut deep, I moved forward. Another chapter of survival.

A month later, I received a voicemail from Judy. She wanted to know if I had taken another job—they were interested in meeting with me again!

Without hesitation, I arranged another meeting, explaining that while I had accepted another position, I hadn't been there long, and I was interested in finding a way to make things work with Lasell Village. The irony was not lost on me—it felt almost laughable, like Cinderella politely declining the ball because she had "other plans."

By the time the interview rolled around, I was meticulously prepared, as was my standard. I wore my finest navy-blue suit, hair sleek in a tight French roll, nails perfectly manicured, and makeup subtle but polished. The pearl necklace was the final touch that brought everything together, completing the look I had so carefully curated over time.

With my trusted Bally pumps and brand-new leather valise—pristine, stylish, and professional—sealed the deal. Each element of my outfit was chosen deliberately to project the image of a serious businesswoman: confident, poised, and completely in control. Together, these pieces weren't just accessories; they were the embodiment of my commitment to success and my careful attention to detail.

In my hands, I carried a fresh pad of paper with questions carefully plotted. I wasn't just attending an interview—I was taking charge. This time, Steve would face a different version of me, one who was poised and resolute, fully aware of what was at stake. I was ready.

There was no room for doubt now.

The interview was carefully staged, and I was acutely aware of the proprieties, both explicit and implicit. With my leather portfolio prominently placed on the desk, we began. I deliberately opened the portfolio and took my Watermark ballpoint pen to paper, signaling my official readiness. Armed with a list of twenty-one questions, I was set to be the interviewer. Steve responded well, recognizing the decorum and meticulous preparation that marked my approach—ready for an engaging exchange.

While the details of the interview remain vivid in my memory, success often hinges on a deep awareness of propriety and the art of graceful, deliberate engagement. Mastering this refined skill fosters a primal desire to practice it as often as circumstances permit.

The sense of euphoria that follows is like the exhilaration felt by great athletes or virtuoso musicians after a flawless performance—a powerful, exhilarating triumph of skill, finesse, and strategy. This feeling of accomplishment comes from the seamless integration of preparation, timing, and execution, creating a moment of pure mastery that is both thrilling and rewarding.

The thrill of realizing how well the interview had gone was electrifying! The exceptional offer—an unrivaled salary, bonuses, and benefits package that surpassed anything I'd yet encountered— underscored the immense value Lasell Village executives saw in me. The rush of accomplishment and relief at securing such a prestigious position was invigorating. It was clear that Lasell Village and I were aligned, and I was poised to deliver world-class salesmanship and professionalism. This opportunity promised a solid foundation for mutual success. I felt I found my place among individuals who not only respected me but whom I also deeply respected. We were truly on the same page.

. . .

Amid the professional triumphs, my thoughts often turned to Rachel and the challenges she faced at such a young age. The instability of our lives was accented by the absence of a father, a dysfunctional family, and my limited education made it all the more difficult. Yet, I was determined to give Rachel opportunities I never had.

Enrolling her at Westgate Christian Academy, an evangelical, Christ-centered school on the campus of Westgate Church, felt like the right step forward. Just a town over from Newton, Westgate provided a solid academic foundation in a nurturing environment.

Mary Rydeout, the school's principal, became an invaluable partner throughout this journey. Together, we spent countless hours assessing Rachel's readiness for kindergarten. Ms. Rydeout's kindness and understanding were unmatched, securing generous scholarships to ensure financial challenges didn't hinder Rachel's progress. Although Rachel's late birthday delayed her transition from preschool to kindergarten, her boundless joy for play and the affection she garnered from her little friends were telling signs of her potential. She may not have been ready for academic challenges just yet, but her radiant spirit and warmth showed she was blossoming in her own time.

Rachel's playful nature stood out in every environment, a bright contrast to the seriousness inherent in my life spent working to hold our lives together. Two little brothers at the preschool vied for Rachel's affection, and the younger of the two, zany James, who won her heart with his mischievous humor and ability to make her laugh. His carefree nature perfectly matched Rachel's love for fun. While she adored Matthew, the more composed and academic older brother, Rachel's natural gravitation toward joy and playfulness reflected her cheerful and lively essence.

In many ways, Rachel was the perfect counterpoint to my serious, controlled, and focused demeanor—her exuberance and playful nature complemented my more intense, methodical approach to life. Where I found solace in structure and concentration, Rachel thrived in spontaneous and joyful moments, enriching our lives with her infectious energy and laughter.

Westgate Christian Academy was a true blessing, providing me with the peace of mind I needed to concentrate on my work each day while Rachel flourished in a nurturing and secure environment. The academy instilled a deep sense of pride in its students, who wore their prestigious uniforms with honor. It was more than just an institution; it was a place where Rachel engaged with her early development, learned about Jesus, and participated in worship and fellowship with her classmates. The active involvement of parents in the church on weekends further enriched this community, creating a spiritually fulfilling and holistic experience.

Meanwhile, the Lasell Village management company was diligently courting potential financiers for development and tirelessly worked to secure deposits from future residents. This daily grind was made more manageable by the positive synergy among my colleagues. We found solace in each other's company, as we shared an open 1,000-square-foot workspace overlooking a picturesque New England neighborhood. The scene outside, with its sidewalks lined by majestic oak trees, rustic shrubs, and a sea of green, perfectly framed the quintessential New England charm of Colonial, Tudor, and Shingle-style homes beneath a canopy of blue skies.

The camaraderie among Judy, Aileen, and me was a constant source of joy as we pursued potential buyers with enthusiasm and laughter. While there was a healthy dose of competitiveness and occasional upstaging, we deeply respected each other's strengths. We often adapted one another's inventive strategies to forge our own unique approaches.

The term "teamwork" is inadequate to describe our dynamic. Teamwork was more than a concept there; it was a shared philosophy. Despite our diverse passions and backgrounds, we united with a singular goal: success. It was fascinating to witness the synergy among three women—one Irish, one Italian, and one Jewish—working in harmony each day, proving that unity transcends cultural differences and fuels extraordinary accomplishment.

Our relationship was a sisterhood steeped in mutual respect, where even our most elaborate flimflam presentations were met with a transparent understanding that cut through pretense. At times, I playfully sparred with Judy, teasing her by claiming to be more Jewish than she was—a comment that left her profoundly astonished. My studies in Hebrew and my growing understanding of Jewish traditions and customs allowed me to gain a solid grasp of the meaning of "kosher" food and other Jewish concepts. This sparked lively debates with Judy, whose father, I believe, had been a kosher butcher, deepening our discussions and offering rich perspectives on the subject.

These exchanges were always in good fun, yet I often felt as if Judy were a long-lost relative—one who, though not technically in my family tree, played an intrinsic part in my life.

Eventually, we reached a plateau in our objectives. With time slipping away, we needed a breakthrough to propel us forward. The mounting pressure was palpable, and we risked losing momentum. In response, our managing director, Steve, convened a high-stakes brainstorming session. This conference offered an opportunity to explore best practices and innovative ideas to drive us beyond our current impasse. No idea was too unconventional. Our challenge was to conjure something substantial from mere possibilities, transforming potential into actionable success.

High-stakes brainstorming? Pressure? No idea too unconventional?

These directives were music to my ears. I proposed a bold strategy: a groundbreaking ceremony designed to seize the spotlight and create a buzz. I pictured a grand event featuring the mayor, local newspapers, and all our prospects, turning every moment into an opportunity for maximum impact. It was the quintessential "fake it till you make it" approach. With Steve and my colleagues intrigued, I continued: "Let's rent some striking heavy equipment—easy enough. Transform the site into an enticing showcase, then invite our prospects back to the office for a sophisticated soirée complete with champagne and exquisite hors d'oeuvres."

And just like that, we had the catalyst we needed—and a touch of fun to boot.

The event was a resounding success. People began placing their deposits, and we managed to propel Lasell Village, the town of Auburndale, and Lasell College toward a brighter future.

From observing the indomitable Betty Kraus and my enterprising parents, I learned the essence of an unwavering, can-do attitude and the relentless pursuit of goals. My colleagues often thought I was audacious, even a bit eccentric, in my efforts to connect with potential buyers. Channeling Betty's sales techniques, I handled one particular case with remarkable success. Mr. Martalo was a former professor who, with his wife, attended every event and invitation that featured food of any quality or quantity. Many assumed he was merely a connoisseur of fine cuisine, perhaps too frugal to consider one of our apartments.

I, however, saw things differently and persisted in my belief that Mr. Martalo and his wife were serious prospects. In the end, my conviction proved correct—they purchased not one, but two adjacent apartments, creating an expansive penthouse and securing the largest sale we had achieved to date.

• • •

My years in Massachusetts at Lasell Village and with my colleagues was truly cherished. They were nothing short of wonderful. Life brimmed with excitement and new experiences for Rachel and me, each day an adventure waiting to unfold. On weekends, Rachel donned her beloved "Quincy Market" dress, poised to dance to any melody that came her way. Whether it was classical music, a violinist, a pianist, or the end credits of a film, Rachel was ready, moving with an ethereal grace that captivated everyone around her. Her soft, blonde curls and angelic movements drew admiring gazes wherever she went, turning every moment into a magical display of joy and beauty.

Reflecting on those tender moments, I am reminded of Rachel's profound connection to music. I recall a time when she was barely a year old and still too young to speak, Rachel was deeply moved by the melodies that surrounded her. We once wandered into Faneuil Hall, where a performance of *West Side Story* was in full swing. The song "Maria," which my stepfather also cherished, brought Rachel to tears. Was it an early, instinctive yearning for the poignant call of the tenor, or was it simply a manifestation of her innate sensitivity and loving nature? Whatever was the source of these tears, Rachel was special. I held her close, offering comfort and reassurance, marveling at the depth of her early tenderness. It was both bewildering and heartwarming to witness such profound emotion from someone so small.

Every birthday was a grand event, each with its own theme, but one of Rachel's favorites was her pirate party. I still recall the excitement of one child calling the number on the invitation, shouting, "I can come! I can come!"—pure innocence, pure joy. The young child didn't even mention Rachel's name. She was just eager to join in. Hosting those special days brought such joy for the children and parents. There was something magical about watching the children revel in these moments of simple joy.

If there was a scorecard for motherhood, I'd have filled it out every day, evaluating myself on every aspect of Rachel's well-being. Was she happy? Was she healthy, well-adjusted? Was I doing enough to satisfy the roles of mother and father? Was she learning about the love of her Heavenly Father? Was she being challenged mentally and physically? Did she feel loved? I constantly measured myself against the future I hoped she'd have, wanting to ensure she grew into a well-rounded, healthy adult.

We shared so many treasured moments together. We saw all the great movies—*Toy Story, Fantasia, Babe: Pig in the City*—watching them over and over, laughing and crying in equal measure. We read *The Wind in the Willows, The Velveteen Rabbit*, and *Charlotte's Web* repeatedly, savoring every word as if they were new each time. But our happiest times were spent outdoors—long walks by the beach in every season, Rachel doing endless cartwheels under the sun and shade. Christmases were magical, and Halloween was a beloved event. I became whatever she needed—mother, father, sister—all wrapped into one.

Of course, not every moment was idyllic. Rachel's allergy attacks were a constant struggle, especially during winter. There were hospitalizations, like the time Ms. Rydeout called me at work to come for Rachel, who was walking around in a daze with a dangerously high fever. Her severe allergies persisted despite my fervent hope that she'd outgrow them. I spent countless hours researching, consulting immunologists across the country, reading white papers, studying the intricacies of deficient immune systems. It was a relentless pursuit driven by love and a desire to ease my daughter's suffering.

When the insurance settlement from the California auto accident finally came, we celebrated with a much-needed vacation to Disney World. The night we left, it was freezing in Boston, and Rachel was exhausted. We rented a red convertible Mustang, and the moment we dropped the top and felt the warm, balmy Orlando breeze, something shifted. We both came alive. cruising down the road, and Rachel turned to me, her face glowing, and said those unforgettable words: "I love you, Mom!"

Time passed, and Lasell Village blossomed into a remarkable success. Amidst this professional triumph, I continued my tireless quest to find answers to Rachel's health challenges. After what felt like endless research and consultations, Rachel's pediatrician and I reached what seemed the best possible solution: a change in climate. A dry environment, like that found in California, with its minimal vegetation and reduced exposure to mold and allergens, seemed worth a try. It was a glimmer of hope in an otherwise exhausting battle with her allergies.

The timing felt serendipitous. I had once again sold myself out of a job. Lasell Village was a rewarding chapter, but I knew it was time to turn the page. After years of diligently repairing my credit and saving every penny, I was finally ready to take the leap into the financial services industry—a new horizon that promised both challenge and opportunity.

So, we geared up to return to California, its drier climate and potential for a fresh start causing the state to appear to be the perfect place to begin anew. This time, I had direction, a roadmap—not just for my career, but for finding balance within my family. It was a rare chance to move forward and heal the past, reconcile the gaps, and create something better for Rachel and me.

My last day at Lasell Village stirred something deep within me that touched the core of my being. I wasn't just saying goodbye to a job—it was the heart-wrenching realization that I would never again call New England home. This marked the end of an era that shaped me into the person I had become. It was the closing of a chapter in my personal, unspoken education—the kind that life itself imparts, teaching you lessons about responsibility, integrity, and how to craft a meaningful life. These were not lessons learned in classrooms, but in the trenches of real-world experience, where every challenge brought wisdom and every triumph added to the person I had evolved into.

As I bid my farewell to Judy, something unexpected happened. I began to sob, and I couldn't stop. The flood of emotion was overwhelming. It wasn't just Judy I would miss, but also the entire essence of New England—its rhythm and soul, the life I had built there. Yet, even as I left, I knew New England would forever reside in my heart, shaping and guiding my future.

FROM MOB TIES TO MIRACLES

CHAPTER 14

FAITH AND SAN DIEGO: RACHEL'S BAPTISM, A NEAR MISS ON 9/11, AND MY MOTHER'S LAST GOODBYE

RACHEL AND I RETURNED TO CALIFORNIA WITH EVERY intention of making it our final home. The weather was always beautiful, which brought Rachel immense relief of her allergies disappearing. We were healthy, optimistic, and ready to embrace whatever came our way. Sundays became sacred as we faithfully attended church, and Wednesdays were equally cherished for Bible study. More than a routine, our Sundays and Wednesdays were rituals that gave our week structure, hope, and joy.

Wednesday nights always began at Souplantation. We'd arrive just before the dinner rush, and the place would already be humming with energy—adults chatting, children laughing, and everyone pushing their trays through the colorful parade of fresh salads. The buffet was endless, filled with excited kids who slowed the line, captivated by the endless choices. Rachel loved it there and always made multiple trips for more soup or sweet treats.

The atmosphere was simple, yet fulfilling. It promised more than food; it poured out comfort and the joy of shared moments, the perfect setting to quietly prepare mentally for the night ahead at Bible study. Afterward, we often wandered into the Christian bookstore at church, searching for a small trinket or treasure to complement the evening. These were the moments that made life feel complete— simple, wholesome, and full of meaning.

One Wednesday night during service, the pastor made a stirring altar call. It was a powerful, unmistakable moment—like something out of a Billy Graham crusade—in which the weight of eternity hung in the air. No one wanted to be left behind. His words were simple, yet profound, resonating with the hearts of everyone in the room, even the youngest. I glanced over at Rachel, not yet seven years old. She sat up straight, her eyes wide with a seriousness beyond her years. Perched on the edge of her seat, she was poised and ready, her little spirit clearly stirred.

"Whoa!" I thought, in awe of the Holy Spirit moving in my sweet Rachel. "Come now, don't hesitate!" the pastor called out. "Make your decision to follow Jesus." I watched as that call reached directly into Rachel's heart. Without a second of doubt, she jumped to her feet and, with determined steps, walked to the altar, ready to make her public profession of faith.

I was overwhelmed—not just by Rachel's courage, but by the undeniable presence of the Holy Spirit guiding her. It was an experience that transcended words. The grace of God was so evident, I know a profound, eternal decision was made before my eyes. The joy in my heart was indescribable, and the following week, on September 16, 1999, Rachel was baptized in the Pacific Ocean at La Jolla Shores. That day was a sacred milestone, forever etched in my memory, as the waves of the ocean met the waves of grace in her life.

• • •

San Diego brought a sense of glory and adventure to our lives, a place where every day felt like a new beginning. It was paradise— endless walks along sun-kissed beaches, leisurely strolls through beautiful neighborhoods, and the vibrant energy of the farmers' markets. We wandered for miles through the Del Mar Fairgrounds, soaking in the festive atmosphere. There was no room for boredom;

every corner of the city offered something magical. Rachel, with her love of ballet, thrived. She took ballet lessons, dreaming to dance on her toes. It was a time of light and joy, where the rhythm of life aligned perfectly with our hearts.

I began working on acquiring my life insurance license. Once it was in my hand, I came across an ad for a salesperson-in-training position. That's when I met Kelly Shaw, an independent insurance agent whose booming business was growing rapidly. I was immediately drawn to Kelly's integrity and straightforward approach. He offered me the role and asked me to "babysit" his office while he and his wife took a well-deserved trip he earned for achieving the highest sales volume in the company. Before leaving, he encouraged me to reach out to his clients. If I moved any of them closer to a sale, Kelly would close the deal upon his return, and we'd split the commissions.

By the time Kelly came back, I had five prospects ready to move forward. What I didn't know from my license prep, I quickly learned by studying the meticulously organized brochures Kelly had filed away, each unlocking new insights into the business. It was the start of something exciting, and I could feel momentum building.

Kelly and I began working side by side, and I absorbed everything he had to offer by watching his every move, memorizing his presentations, and infusing my own style into the process. Together, we became an unstoppable team, and soon I was earning an impressive income. My years of experience in the senior living industry had prepared me well for this moment, but the work was less strenuous, and the income potential far exceeded anything I had experienced before. It was as if everything I had learned led me to this point, and the rewards were finally unfolding.

Of course, I was never willing to settle when there was more to explore. As luck would have it, Morgan Stanley had an office conveniently located right next door. Just a ladies' restroom separated our worlds of finance. I decided to expand my credentials and get the full securities training that Kelly didn't offer. So, one day, I casually stepped away from Kelly's office, took a little detour, and popped into Morgan Stanley to inquire about setting up an interview. Lo and behold, they were interested! We scheduled it on the spot. What can I say? Timing is everything.

Days and weeks flew by as I worked with Kelly, racking up commissions and awaiting Morgan Stanley's call. When the call came, the process unfolded in the typical fashion—multiple rounds of interviews, mathematical and ethical exams, reference and credit checks, and fingerprinting. I wasn't in a rush, though. Things were going smoothly with Kelly, and the convenience of having Morgan Stanley right next door made my transition seamless.

Morgan Stanley returned with an offer that was my golden ticket—the opportunity to join their esteemed Wealth Management Financial Advisor Associate Program. This wasn't just any job; it was a three-year, full-time journey designed to transform candidates into top-tier financial advisors. The program was comprehensive, incorporating licensing exams, a structured curriculum, and personalized coaching. It promised to be rigorous, demanding, and intense, pushing me to master the financial landscape.

Upon successfully obtaining the coveted Series 7 and 66 licenses and completing all program requirements, the experience would culminate with three weeks of final training at Morgan Stanley's corporate offices in New York City. This was the pinnacle—a chance to solidify everything I had learned, refine my skills, and become part of a legacy of financial excellence.

It was an offer too thrilling to pass up—who wouldn't accept? The chance to train at Morgan Stanley, one of the most prestigious names in finance, was a once-in-a-lifetime opportunity. It was obviously the next step, and I needed to take it.

So, I sat down with Kelly and, with genuine gratitude, explained that while I loved working for him and had gained so much from our time together, advancing to the next level was calling me. Morgan Stanley's offer, I stated, was simply too good to turn down. Kelly, ever gracious, understood my ambition, and with his blessing, I eagerly accepted Morgan Stanley's generous offer.

• • •

On August 13, 2001, I embarked on my journey with Morgan Stanley. Having already completed my Life and Health Licensing, I was energized and ready to tackle the remaining licensing exams, eager to join the upcoming training class in New York. My colleague, Joy Rizzo, and I planned to stay at the Southgate Towers, just a few miles from the iconic Twin Towers. Rachel would accompany me, attending school nearby while I immersed myself in the rigorous training sessions that awaited.

By this time, Rachel and I had settled in Rancho Bernardo, and I was working from that office. However, Rachel was deeply unsettled by the thought of going to New York. She was only in the third grade, but her distress was so palpable that she went to her teacher in tears, pleading, "I don't want to go to New York." Her teacher called me at work to share just how upset Rachel was. Little did we know, that decision carried with it a sense of foreboding, a harbinger of the dark events that were soon to unfold in the heart of New York City.

The only hurdle that remained was completing my Series 7 exam, which, with a bit of effort, I could finish in time. Eager to go to New York with Joy, I sought the advice of the managing director, hoping for clarity on whether I could join her in the upcoming class. After carefully considering my progress, the director advised me to wait and join the next training session.

Looking back, I can't help but see the hand of divine providence in that moment. What seemed a simple decision at the time—a matter of scheduling—was, in truth, something far greater, a protective grace that watched over Rachel and me. Had I rushed to complete the licensing, we might have been in New York, at the very heart of the storm about to unfold.

On the morning of September 11, 2001, I arrived late to the office. From the moment I stepped inside, something felt off. The air was unnaturally cold, the entire space had been drained of life. The usual hustle and bustle, the casual conversations over coffee, were nowhere to be found. Instead, every eye was fixed on the screens— TVs and computer monitors all flashing the same horrifying images of jets crashing into the Twin Towers on an endless, grim replay.

It was surreal, like stepping into an Alfred Hitchcock film. The atmosphere was laden with an almost surreal shock, as if the world had collectively paused to grapple with its deepest fears. The silence, heavy and unsettling, was sporadically punctured by fragmented, cryptic updates from news anchors, their words conveying an underlying sense of confusion and disbelief. Each disjointed report echoed a shared struggle to comprehend the incomprehensible.

The entire office, the entire nation, was gripped by shock and disbelief. No words were spoken, just stunned faces, each person trying to process what was unfolding before us. Time stood still.

Suddenly, as if waking from a daze, I jumped to my feet, heart pounding. "Oh my God! What about Joy and our other colleagues?" The realization hit me like a wave, yet the room remained still, everyone frozen in front of their screens, locked in disbelief. Hadn't anyone questioned the well-being of our friends?

I moved through the office, shaking my colleagues from their stupor, asking over and over, "Has anyone checked on Joy? What about the others?" But there were no answers—just blank stares, as if the horror unfolding before us had numbed their ability to act. Desperation set in. I grabbed my phone, calling Joy's cell, the hotel, the office in New York—anywhere I could think of—only to be met with dead silence. Finally, someone at the hotel, sounding dazed and disoriented, picked up. They had no idea where anyone was and had no information to offer. The world had stopped. All we could do was hope.

By God's grace, Joy and my colleagues from the training class returned home with horrific stories that would haunt them forever. Joy shared how, after witnessing the first tower being hit, she had ignored the intercom's calm assurances, advising everyone to stay in their offices—that everything would be fine. In that moment, something deep within her took over, a determination to survive. She struck out and began the long descent down seventy-seven floors. Soon, the stairs were a massive, almost synchronized movement—hundreds of people, all moving briskly together, driven by one instinct for survival, flowing like a human river toward safety.

Sadly, not all were as fortunate. The vice president of security, Rick Rescorla, and twelve other Morgan Stanley employees perished that day. Rick, a hero to the end, had stayed behind to ensure others got out, sacrificing his life for theirs. The weight of their loss and the sheer magnitude of the day left a lasting scar on all of us, reminding us of our fragility and the courage of the human spirit.

Meanwhile, my training had been delayed and was now set for San Francisco in a building with a troubling reputation on California Street—a site that had been struck by terrorists years before. The shadow of uncertainty loomed large, and as much as I tried to focus on the next steps in my career, something within me had shifted. I had become disenfranchised with my brokerage future, questioning whether it was worth the cost, not just to me, but also to my daughter.

Rachel, who had once been so vibrant and full of life, was unraveling before my eyes. The stress in our lives had seeped into hers. She began losing her homework, and not just once—twice, wound up in detention. Her expensive jackets vanished at school, and her once careful, responsible nature was fading. I could see it in her eyes— school wasn't holding her attention, and her happiness was slipping away.

The most heartbreaking part was discovering her lunch money crumpled in her pocket at the end of the day. When asked why she hadn't used it, she'd simply shrugged and said she was able to eat without it. Perhaps she saved the money because she knew money was tight, maybe sensing that frugality was necessary. The weight of it all— the uncertainty, the financial strain, and my own dissatisfaction—was affecting her in ways I couldn't control, and it tore at me. It felt as though cracks were forming in the foundation we were building.

Rachel's growing discontent and pushback, coupled with the looming San Francisco trip, made it clear that something had to change. Additionally, Rachel's allergies were beginning to flare again as fall turned to winter, and I could see the toll it was taking on her, both physically and emotionally. My heart ached as I realized that my pursuit of this career, however promising, was coming at too great a cost.

With a renewed sense of determination, I made the decision: I handed in my resignation. It was time to step away from the corporate grind, the relentless demands, and the uncertainty of a future I no longer felt aligned with. Instead, I chose to go solo, to become a sole proprietor. This would give me the freedom and flexibility I needed for my small family. Rachel needed me now more than ever, and I was determined to be there for her.

In that moment, I embraced a new path, one that allowed me to set my own hours, build something on my terms, and, most importantly, be the mother my daughter so desperately needed. It was a leap of faith, but with each step forward, I knew it was the right one.

• • •

At the dawn of 2002, I took a decisive step forward, filing with the Department of Insurance for the name approval of McCormack Financial & Insurance Services. This marked the beginning of a new chapter filled with purpose and ambition. I swiftly became appointed and began forging relationships with top-tier A and A+ insurance wholesalers across the country. My business began to flourish, and clients found me with remarkable ease.

With each successful transaction, my financial stability grew. I set aside substantial commissions, all while focusing on the long-term goal of purchasing a home. It would require a solid two years of consistent income and a sizable down payment, but the promise of homeownership was a beacon of hope guiding my efforts. Each step I took was measured and intentional, driven by a future vision in which my hard work and determination would culminate in a place Rachel and I could call our own.

To formalize my business and secure my family's future, I engaged an attorney and established McCormack Financial & Insurance Services, Inc. This step was crucial in solidifying my professional and personal endeavors. In addition to creating a corporation, I took out a $1 million life insurance policy, ensuring Rachel's financial protection in the event anything happened to me. I also arranged for a trust to be set up, guaranteeing Rachel's financial needs would be met and managed with the utmost care.

During this period, Rachel began expressing a longing for a father figure, particularly with the onslaught of annual father-daughter dances. It was a challenging time, seeing her wish for something that seemed out of reach, but my resolve to provide for her and secure her future remained steadfast.

Regrettably, looking back, my greatest misstep was reaching out to Rachel's father. Given our history, any approach was bound to be jarring. I had sought assistance from social services to locate him, and by a twist of fate, they failed to delete his phone number from their records. To my astonishment, when I dialed the number, he answered. He remembered me immediately and, without a hint of surprise or disbelief, acknowledged that he had a daughter.

In a moment of misguided hope, I handed the phone to Rachel. The anticipation overwhelmed her; her heart raced and threatened to leap from her chest. It was a decision that only compounded the emotional strain she was already under.

That call began the most difficult period of Rachel's childhood. Christopher's deliberate and minimal involvement would have been less damaging had we left well enough alone. It would have been infinitely better for Rachel to continue imagining some distant, idealized figure who might exist somewhere in the universe. She could have envisioned him as a noble presence, untainted by reality. Instead, the truth of his character—a deadbeat from the very first phone call— was a harsh and disheartening revelation.

Painfully and with grave sadness and guilt, I shouldered the responsibility of this misstep. As a genuinely loving mother, I had meticulously crafted every facet of her life, yet I walked her into that life-altering blunder. Where else could the blame lie but with me? I was the sole constant in her life, her only provider and protector. It had been my decision, my choice, that led to that grievous error. If only I had foreseen the misery it would bring, I never would have made that call.

And so, there I was again, standing at the crossroads of regret and resilience—a place that felt all too familiar. The weight of my heavy heart wrapped around me, pulling me toward the need to retreat. I longed to hide beneath the covers, seeking their symbolic sanctuary, wanting to escape the unforgiving chill of reality. But even beneath those folds, there was no true refuge from the inevitable confrontation with life's harsh truths.

It's funny, really, how life spins in circles—how winter insists on taking center stage before spring dares to show up. And yet, in that winter season, I kept wearing that smile, pretending tomorrow would be a little lighter.

That same rhythm of life that kept me moving forward, even as the pieces of my carefully crafted plans scattered around me. I'd come to understand there were no perfect decisions—only ones made in the moment, hoping they'd lead to some semblance of peace. And while I carried the weight of my mistakes, I also carried the belief that life, in its cruel and unpredictable way, still held the chance for redemption.

I had wandered—not far, but far enough to realize no road ever leads quite where you expect. And now, with more years behind me than I cared to count, I could see clearly that life was just a series of cycles. One moment, laughter filled the air, and the next, I was picking up broken pieces. If I learned anything from those foolish years, it was that every high is inevitably followed by a low. And there I was again, standing at the edge of that low, feeling the weight of the fall.

But even then, there was a stubborn flicker of hope—a refusal to stay down for too long. In those moments, I told myself to wait it out, to wait for the dreams that still might come true, even as life handed me yet another lesson in patience. I was tired of trying, but somewhere inside, there was always that tiny voice, whispering, "Keep going."

Eventually, those brighter days did emerge. I found a beautiful Spanish-style California ranch in the San Diego Country Estates, nestled in the serene expanse of Ramona. The community, with its strict HOA rules, preserved the charm of equestrian life while offering a peaceful, country atmosphere. With half an acre to breathe, I felt a renewed sense of hope. Rachel thrived in a sweet, secure elementary school within walking distance, and she formed a treasured friendship with AJ, the kind-hearted girl from across the street. Together, they embarked on a joyful childhood journey.

It was a profound joy to finally have a home of our own, a yearning carried with me from childhood. The peace and comfort of a personal sanctuary is one of life's true delights—an essential part of the human experience. A home defines a family's identity, embodying honor, stability, and pride, all intimately shared within its walls. This new place was perfectly suited to our needs, allowing me to walk Rachel to school each morning and welcome her back each afternoon. It also provided a dedicated office space, where I often worked at 5 a.m. in my pajamas, nursing a cup of coffee and making calls to the East Coast to catch the day's interest rates as early as possible. The three-hour time difference worked in my favor, letting me get work done while Rachel slept and granting me the freedom to fully embrace the simple, cherished moments of family life in the afternoons.

• • •

As life flourished, my thoughts often turned to my mother. She'd undergone heart bypass surgery years earlier due to years of smoking and weight struggles. With Mom growing older, I wanted Rachel to spend as much time with her as possible, especially given the extraordinary bond they shared. That deep connection began when my mother cared for Rachel in her early years and remained remarkable. The love between them was so strong and undeniable that I again entrusted Rachel's care to her grandmother whenever needed.

One day, I drove to pick up Rachel from my mother's house. The sun was shining, not a cloud in the sky—a perfectly ordinary day. As I turned the corner onto Mom's street, I spotted a little girl standing all alone with a sign that read, "Tomatoes 10 cents," written in classic eight-year-old scrawl. I didn't think much of it at first, until I realized— wait a minute—that little entrepreneur was my daughter! Rachel had set up a makeshift table and was standing proudly by the curb, staring right at me with her disarming, effervescent smile. I slammed on the brakes in shock, narrowly avoiding an accident.

There she was, having casually left my mother's house, walked half a block to a busy street corner, and as a sole proprietor was selling tomatoes to strangers like she was running a farmers' market! God only knows how long she had been there, conducting business like a seasoned professional. My heart sank as reality hit me—my mother's health was no longer up to the task of watching Rachel, especially since when she wasn't running her tomato empire, Rachel was performing circus acts in the tree next to the house. Swinging from branches without a care in the world, Rachel had been essentially babysitting herself. And when she got bored? She just invented new adventures, such as selling tomatoes on the corner.

Did life ever leave us in peace? No, fate had other plans. That same year, my mother was diagnosed with lung cancer, a blow that shook our already delicate world. As I juggled making a living, maintaining the house, and raising Rachel, I became deeply involved in my mother's care. Her doctors, by then familiar faces, offered support, but the weight of responsibility fell squarely on my shoulders. Rachel and I visited as often as we could, cherishing the fleeting moments we had, knowing time was slipping through our fingers.

Covered by the shadow of my mother's illness, Rachel and I were determined to embrace life with all the joy we could muster. We ventured to Disneyland with AJ and even tried our hand at flying lessons. That didn't quite go as planned—one flight left us wide-eyed as Rachel's door swung open mid-air, only to be quickly slammed shut by the co-pilot. But that didn't stop us. We just opted for ground-based adventures, walking every beach from Del Mar to La Jolla and spending countless evenings watching the sun dip below the Pacific horizon from every possible vantage point. Summers in San Diego were nothing short of magical.

In March, just before her seventieth birthday, my mother passed away after a long struggle with congestive heart failure, finding peace at last as she went to be with the Lord. Even in her final days, she fought with every ounce of strength she had, refusing to surrender. Looking back, how could I blame her? It was in her nature, as is the nature of all women in our family—we were survivors, resilient to the core. We bargained with God for more time, another day, another year, another chance to fully live, no matter how hard the fight. It's who we were, and in her, I recognized the wellspring of the same fierce will I carried in myself.

FROM MOB TIES TO MIRACLES

CHAPTER 15

RISING THROUGH THE THORNS: TRIUMPH OVER BETRAYAL, LAUNCHING RACHEL, AND NEW BEGINNINGS

As Rachel completed sixth grade, I was at a crossroads. She was set to transition into the Ramona High School district, a stark contrast to the sheltered, insular environment of her small country school. The prospect filled me with unease. The district's graduating classes ranked dismally low in the state, and I knew Rachel wouldn't be challenged academically as she deserved. Homeschooling was out of the question given my demanding work schedule, and the more I thought about it, the more precarious our future felt.

At the same time, the personal loss of my sister Mary weighed heavily on me. Her tragic death from alcoholism was a sobering reminder of how quickly life can spiral out of control. It added to the uncertainty and sense of fragility already building inside me. Compounding this was the Cedar Fire, one of the most destructive wildfires California had ever seen, which came perilously close to our home in the Estates, nearly wiping out everything we had. The devastation around us was a wake-up call, and I wasn't ready or willing to face these uncertainties again. It was time to reimagine our future and carve a new path forward.

I sold the Ramona house for nearly double what I had paid and moved to Carmel Valley, a picturesque suburb of San Diego just east of Del Mar. The decision aimed at ensuring Rachel the stability she needed after years of moving from place to place. Carmel Valley would be her home from seventh grade through high school graduation—a place where she could grow and develop into a well-adjusted young adult. The community was filled with families that reflected the aspirational nature of Southern California life: stay-at-home moms and fathers who were lawyers, CEOs, doctors, engineers, chemists, and entrepreneurs. It was an environment in which success was the expectation, and the competition was implicit in every interaction. I knew Rachel would be surrounded by peers from families who valued education and ambition, giving her the foundation she needed to thrive in a world that demanded excellence.

Her first two years in junior high were a period of adjustment, and her grades reflected the struggle. She wasn't on track for university acceptance, and the risk of her falling behind her peers weighed heavily on both of us. Many evenings were spent sitting together, praying and trying to get to the heart of her academic issues. I needed to understand what would reignite her drive and up her game. It became clear—she needed a mission, a sense of purpose beyond the classroom.

Her heart was set on ballet, a desire to dance on pointe and embody the grace and discipline that came with it. Though money was tight, I enrolled her in ballet classes twice a week. It was an investment, but a worthwhile one. The transformation was immediate—Rachel thrived, embracing the refined structure and pursuit of excellence that ballet demanded. Watching her pour herself into this new passion, I knew I had made the right choice. I supported her every step of the way, knowing that sometimes, purpose and passion are as important as academics.

While Rachel danced away, I joined Merrill Lynch's San Diego office, drawn by the promise of a stable income and the robust support services that had increasingly strained my own business. It was invigorating to be part of a world-class organization once more. During a meeting with my HR officer, I confided my feelings of underachievement as a woman in the field. She glanced around the room—a sea of men in navy blue suits—and asked, "How many women do you see?" My response was candid: "None." It was a stark reminder of the gender disparity, but also a validation of the unique space I occupied.

At Merrill Lynch, I dedicated myself wholeheartedly to my work, earning recognition as a Top Advisor and consistently ranking in the highest quintiles for annualized growth. My role involved acquiring new clients and expertly structuring their equity and bond portfolios, annuities, mutual funds, and various life insurance products. I even marked the Dow Jones Industrial Average at 12,621 on January 24 on my calendar—an echo of a bygone era, yet a testament to my enduring journey.

• • •

For years, my life was devoted to raising Rachel, nurturing our bond, and ensuring her safety and happiness. I focused on fostering a stable and supportive environment for her, cherishing every moment as she grew into a young woman. As I watched her strength and maturity blossom, I began to feel the time was right to explore new possibilities for myself. With this newfound sense of readiness, I ventured into the world of dating. I joined several online dating sites, taking tentative steps toward discovering a new chapter in my life, while protecting my precious bond with Rachel.

One night, I pulled out my collection of wigs and hairpieces—because who doesn't dream of more hair, right?—while preparing for a night of dancing. One of Rachel's friends, Christabel, looked at me with wide-eyed curiosity and offered this priceless advice: "Mrs. McCormack, why don't you date a black man?" she asked. "They love wigs on women!" Her candor and infectious laughter were a breath of fresh air. I should have told her, "I would, but your father is already taken."

There were delightful moments when I begged Rachel and Christabel to let me do their makeup. Once, they consented, and oh, did they sparkle with ruby lipstick and matching rouge cheeks!

We were a scene out of a fairytale, with Rachel, Christabel, and me, dressed up like ladies off to the ball. With Rachel by my side, I could indulge in the childlike joy I never fully embraced and never wanted to outgrow.

The funniest dating experiences I had were truly sitcom-worthy. There was the time I walked up to a French restaurant, eagerly anticipating a romantic rendezvous, only to find a short, portly man sitting on the bench outside. He was just shy of five feet tall, grinning like he'd just won the lottery. His photo promised something entirely different, and I seriously considered taking up residence in the restaurant's coat closet to avoid dealing with this face-to-face surprise. But it was too late. He recognized me. Then there was the gentleman who used a photo of himself that was three decades old—clearly hoping I wouldn't notice the passage of time between then and now.

One date after another, the stories were equally outrageous: men who spent the entire evening pining over their ex-wives, relying on me to be a sympathetic ear for their unresolved romantic drama. It felt like I was auditioning for a role in *Misfits of California*, the hit show in which the leading man was always a questionable choice. Yet, despite the absurdity, every night dancing swept me into a dream of romance, as if the universe might just surprise me with a fairy tale ending amid all the lunacy.

As time marched on, I crossed paths with a delightful Italian gentleman. He was a civil engineer with his own thriving business, who possessed a comedic flair that could brighten even the gloomiest of days. Originally from New Zealand, Joe Romano's humor was a captivating blend of dry English wit and sharp, intelligent observations. With my every laugh, my every girlish grin, and every genuine chuckle, his humor flourished, as if it drew energy from our shared amusement.

Joe's townhome was less than a mile from my apartment, making our meetings effortlessly enjoyable. Though he harbored a longing for children, life's timing thwarted that dream. Yet, the escapades of laughter we shared were a refreshing reminder of how joy could be found even in unexpected places.

As our relationship deepened, each moment we spent together

made it increasingly clear that we were moving toward something meaningful. After a year of exclusive dating, he proposed, offering Rachel and me a reprieve from the financial strains of single parenthood and a genuine partnership. His commitment extended beyond mere promises; he pledged to be a steadfast presence in our lives, encompassing not only our emotional well-being but also contributing to Rachel's college education. He expressed a heartfelt desire to be a true father and husband, filling a role he had always longed for but never had the chance to embrace.

Reassured by his sincere intentions, I accepted his proposal, embracing the promise of a shared future. We celebrated our nuptials with a small gathering of close friends at Orfila Vineyards, a picturesque winery owned by one of Joe's best friends. The venue, surrounded by lush vineyards and rolling hills, perfectly captured the essence of our commitment. As we exchanged vows, the air was filled with joy and hope, a beautiful blending of our families and dreams, a moment we would cherish.

As I nurtured my close bond with Rachel, we cherished our many private walks, enjoyed special dinners at fine restaurants, and engaged in heartfelt conversations to ensure she was thriving. Our adventures even took us to Lake Arrowhead, just the two of us, creating memories that would last a lifetime. When Joe invited us to New Zealand to meet his family, it opened up a world of international travel for Rachel and me.

We marveled at the pristine beaches and endless blue skies surrounding his stunning apartment on the Nelson boardwalk. The views were breathtaking—crystal-clear water lapped against powdery white sands, framed by swaying palm trees. From the harbor, we watched large cargo ships come and go, their journeys expertly guided by harbor master tugboats ushering them into port. It felt like a dream, a vivid contrast to our previous lives, and Joe took great pleasure in sharing this beautiful world with us.

When Rachel entered ninth grade, I resigned from Merrill with a singular mission: to prepare Rachel for college. This was not just a phase; it was an all-consuming pursuit, and I wanted nothing more than to see her succeed. I was determined that she wouldn't face the same challenges I had endured. I would fight tooth and nail, beg, borrow, or do whatever it took to ensure she had every opportunity to thrive. Nothing would stand in my way—I was driven by an unwavering commitment to her future, ready to unleash every ounce of my strength to get her there.

Rachel paid attention as her classmates eagerly discussed the colleges they aspired to attend. This shift marked a turning point for her; suddenly, her academic performance became fiercely competitive. She immersed herself in dance and flourished in her classes, revealing a newfound confidence and determination. I witnessed her transformation from a young girl into a remarkable young lady, eagerly urging me to help her navigate driving school so she could earn her license. It was heartening to see her ambition mirror my own, a true chip off the old block, forging her path with the relentless drive I had instilled in her.

At seventeen, Rachel embarked on the challenging journey of taking practice SATs, fully aware that her scores fell short of our aspirations. Determined to bridge that gap, I hired a private tutor. Rachel embraced the tutoring sessions with remarkable dedication, pouring her heart and soul into her studies. Sometimes she emerged from her room, her eyes reflecting sheer exhaustion, confessing that her brain felt utterly fried. Despite the physical and mental toll, she refused to back down. This wasn't just about passing tests; Rachel was resolutely crafting her future, striving to become an exceptional candidate for the university of her dreams—not settling for anything less. Her industrious efforts were a testament to her ambition, as she meticulously designed a life filled with purpose and promise.

It was electrifying to witness Rachel's ambition, and I embraced my role as her personal coach, channeling every ounce of my energy into refining her path, praying for her success, and shepherding her every step of the way. Our college tours began in October 2010, taking us to captivating destinations like Asheville, North Carolina; Columbia, South Carolina; and Santa Barbara, California.

Graduation day had finally arrived. The college decision was made, and Rachel was eagerly anticipating the chance to celebrate this milestone with her father, who had been invited to share in her achievement. However, the day took an absurd turn when Christopher, unable to rent a car due to his revoked driver's license—a result of his substantial child support arrears—brazenly asked if he could drive my car instead.

His request was both baffling and infuriating, given his unlicensed status and the obvious legal and personal risks involved. When I firmly refused, he reacted with anger, further underscoring his consistent disregard for accountability and his inability to grasp the responsibilities he had neglected for so long.

This incident perfectly encapsulated Christopher's attitude toward responsibility—sidestepping the consequences of his actions and expecting others to accommodate his failures without question. It was emblematic of the very dynamic that had defined his role in Rachel's life: a pattern of neglect paired with misplaced entitlement.

At Christmas, Joe invited us to New Zealand for a summer getaway, where we found ourselves seated at the dining table of his stunning apartment, our hearts racing as we prepared to broach a delicate subject. With Rachel to my right and Joe to my left, the time had come to discuss Rachel's college financing. My pulse raced as I steeled myself to address the matter, fully aware of Joe's frugality and the stakes involved.

Trying to seize the moment of vacation bliss to soften the conversation, I took a deep breath and began. "Joe," I said, "I've been diligently preparing Rachel for college, and as you know, we need to discuss how to fund it. Given my financial constraints and her likely ineligibility for need-based scholarships due to your substantial income, I need to explore our options." My heart pounded in my chest, each beat echoing the gravity of the request I was about to make.

To my astonishment, Joe responded without a hint of hesitation or remorse. His answer came slowly, drawn out with an almost theatrical "Naaahhhh," as he shook his head with firm resolve. "No, I can't help. I have my nieces and nephews to support," he said. His unwavering dismissal cut through the air, a stark betrayal we didn't see coming.

I was struck numb, grappling with the crushing blow of Joe's words and how to mitigate the damage they inflicted on my beloved daughter. In that moment, my feelings for him hardened into a deep, consuming loathing. I wished fervently for him to vanish from our lives, his betrayal so raw and unforgivable that it seemed to taint everything he touched. Joe had deceived us both and though I had never known such hatred before, he had become a figure I could no longer tolerate.

Rachel and I sought solace at a charming family pub, a refuge from the wreckage of our shattered expectations. The weight of Joe's refusal was a devastating explosion that left us in the smoldering ruins of our dreams. I held Rachel close, reassuring her that college was still within reach, even if the path was obscured by uncertainty. I vowed that I would find a way, no matter how daunting, and we placed our trust in God for a miracle. In that quiet moment, amidst the clinking of glasses and murmurs of comfort, I promised her that our hope and faith would guide us through the storm.

My relationship with Joe was always strained, marked by an undercurrent of tension and discord. From the very beginning, even the simplest interactions—whether about meals, events, or future plans—were battlegrounds. Joe was, in every sense, a miser. He was unwilling to pay even the smallest amount extra, obsessively seeking out savings, willing to drive across town to save a few cents on a tomato. His world was framed through his narrow, uncompromising lens, where everything was filtered through his own desires and needs.

Initially, Joe stated that my daughter would be the daughter he never had, but when the reality of taking on that responsibility set in, resentment slowly took root. The weight of caring for a child, the sacrifices it entailed, and the demands childrearing made seemed to overwhelm his self-centered nature. Joe's warm words about embracing Rachel as his own gradually transformed into bitterness. It was no surprise that his first marriage ended quickly, and that he remained childless—his world had always been about himself, and he simply couldn't reconcile that with the reality of sharing it with another.

One particularly disturbing incident went beyond selfishness. Joe took his computer in for repairs, and upon returning, he mentioned that the store's management raised concerns about inappropriate images on his device. Without hesitation, he suggested that Rachel was responsible, insinuating that she had been looking at "bad things" online.

Rachel was heartbroken by the accusation. She vehemently denied it, explaining that she rarely, if ever, used his computer, and would never search for anything inappropriate. Watching her cry, overwhelmed by guilt she didn't deserve, was excruciating. I held her as she sobbed, doing my best to comfort her, telling her again and again that I believed her. But the damage had been done—Joe's baseless blame had turned our home into a battleground of mistrust, and no matter how hard I tried to shield her, Rachel was left devastated by his cruelty. It was a nightmare, one that exposed just how fractured our lives with him had become in a matter of four years.

· · ·

Resolved to earn money for Rachel's education, I re-entered the job force, taking a job in Los Angeles and Orange Counties that required me to stay over some nights during the week. Upon returning, Joe would be delighted in answering how famously he and Rachel were getting along, so as to ease my mind when she was alone with him.

One afternoon, I came home earlier than usual and noticed a small Post-it note on Joe's black notebook. At first glance, it seemed insignificant, but upon closer inspection, I realized it contained specific URLs—deliberately written and unmistakably intentional. Something inside me told me to check.

With a deep breath, I typed in the addresses, one by one, and was met with content that left me utterly horrified. What I discovered was far darker than I could have imagined. My heart pounded as I processed the gravity of what I was seeing. A deep unsettling fear took root in me, and I found myself questioning my daughter's safety when she was alone with him.

Then, a surge of urgency took over. My primary instinct was

to protect Rachel and myself at all costs. This was more than just a troubling discovery—it was a turning point. I hurriedly copied the note, securing every shred of evidence. There was no room for hesitation; things were going to get ugly very quickly, and I needed to be prepared for what was to come. This morphed beyond a matter of betrayal to a question of safety, and I wasn't taking any chances.

Over the next few days, unbeknownst to Joe, I discreetly launched an investigation. I reached out to legal authorities and consulted with experts, determined to uncover the full extent of Joe's criminal behavior. I spent hours on the phone, meticulously explaining the situation to those who could help, knowing I had to tread carefully to ensure Joe remained oblivious.

Quietly, I resigned from my job to give the situation my full attention. As Child Protective Services delved into the disturbing evidence, their interest was immediately piqued. They hadn't yet provided me with the next steps, but one thing was certain—Joe was in deep trouble, and it was only a matter of time before the consequences of his actions caught up to him. Along with protecting Rachel and myself, I was setting the stage for justice to be served.

By the weekend, I had carefully calculated my next move. Saturday morning, I was ready—dressed and prepared for the confrontation that would change everything. Calmly but firmly, I asked Joe to sit down, explaining that we needed to discuss something very important.

With deliberate precision, I pulled out the original Post-it note he'd foolishly left behind. The moment he saw it, panic swept over him. His eyes widened in shock, and without hesitation, he lunged forward, snatching it from my hand and bolting to the bathroom to flush it down the toilet. But I was unshaken. I anticipated his every move.

"I made copies," I said coldly, my voice steady as I watched the color drain from his face. "I know exactly what you've been up to, and I've spoken to people who are very interested in this." I paused, letting the gravity of my words sink in. "You're probably going to jail, Joe."

At that moment, the tables had turned entirely. He was no longer in control of his secrets—*I* was. His future was no longer his own, and he knew it. All his arrogance, his manipulations, and his deceit had crumbled, leaving him cornered. For the first time, I held all the power.

The moment I mentioned the possibility of jail, his entire demeanor collapsed. Joe, once so arrogant and self-assured, began to beg for my forgiveness, his voice trembling with fear. He curled into a pathetic fetal position, the reality of his downfall crashing into him. His prestigious position in downtown San Diego's civil engineering world meant nothing now. His greatest concern was the impending consequences of his actions.

"I'm sure they'll be reaching out to me next week," I said, watching him shrink in terror at the thought of his carefully constructed life unraveling.

And I was right. The authorities came to the house the very next afternoon, just as I had anticipated. They informed me they were planning a full forensic investigation of Joe's computers. But Joe, ever the coward, had already destroyed them all and replaced them with a brand-new laptop by Monday. He was desperate to cover his tracks, but it was too late.

I made his life as difficult as possible from that moment on, knowing exactly who he was. Every act of cruelty, every lie he had ever told, stood exposed. I saw the depths of his deceit, and there was no more room for mercy. The man who once boasted about his success and power was exposed to be a cheap, deplorable excuse for a human being, and I was determined to see him face the full weight of his actions.

I couldn't get Rachel and myself out of that house fast enough. Every second we stayed felt like poison, and I knew our escape had to be swift and resolute. I made it a point to turn this nightmare into a teaching moment for Rachel. I sat her down and, with unwavering conviction, telling her, "Never—no, never—allow a man, or anyone for that matter, treat you like this. You are worth more, and I am doing this for us. My actions, my strength, are for your future but mine are secondary."

Determined to make our exit not just a flight, but a triumph, I sought out the finest attorney I could find. He was not only brilliant but deeply sympathetic to what had happened to Rachel and me. With his guidance, I felt empowered, back in control of a situation that seemed overwhelming.

The settlement was substantial—impressive, even. But more than the financial victory, it was a victory of principle. We walked away not as victims, but as survivors who refused to be diminished by betrayal or deceit. Rachel saw, in real time, what it meant to stand tall in the face of adversity, and I knew that the strength I had summoned in those moments provided a lesson she would carry with her forever.

We relocated to a temporary apartment on the beach in Del Mar, where the soothing rhythm of the waves became our soundtrack for healing and renewal. The ocean breeze brought with it a sense of peace and clarity as we focused not on the past but on the future, full speed ahead. It was a time to collect ourselves, to rediscover our strength, and to look forward with hope. Rachel was soon heading off to UC Santa Barbara. Before that pivotal moment, we made one last trip to New England to create a final shared memory before the next chapter.

• • •

On September 18, 2011, Rachel officially started her journey at UC Santa Barbara. I still recall the excitement of the long drive, the joy of getting her new clothes, and the bittersweet task of helping her settle into her dorm. When the time came to say goodbye, we shared a warm embrace, and then—just like that—she disappeared into the swirl of college life, like a ghost fading into a new world.

The drive back to San Diego was endless, stretching out in front of me not only in miles but in emotion. It was a long, lonely journey—made worse by the seemingly never-ending road construction on the 5 Freeway. But even in the midst of that exhausting drive, I knew that this was the beginning of something grand for Rachel, and for me, the close of one chapter and the opening of another.

The following week, I reached out to my dear friend Evelyn Feldman, a kindred spirit I'd met while sitting at a bar in Del Mar.

We had instantly bonded over the bittersweet realization that we were a couple of has-beens—two single women who, under different circumstances, would have been sharing stories about our kids instead of nursing our solitude over cocktails.

Evelyn often came by my apartment, and we'd sit for hours, shooting the breeze and commiserating about how the world had dealt us the short end of the stick. We lamented the distance from our children, the quiet agony of missing them as they ventured into their own lives. With a bottle of wine between us, we'd chatted endlessly, laughing and mourning in equal measure until the wine was gone and these two petite women, barely 100 pounds soaking wet, were too tired to stand. Those simple evenings were a balm—an escape from the loneliness and a reminder that we weren't facing life alone.

But when Monday morning came, the weight of reality hit hard. The sting of sending Rachel off to college lingered, my eyes were still swollen from crying, and the apartment was a hollow echo of the home it once was. I sat in the eerie quiet, as my home adjusted to the absence of Rachel's presence. In the stillness, I wondered what my life would look like from now on. What would I do? Where would I go? For the first time in my life, there was no urgent to-do list, no pressing agenda. My calendar, once filled to the brim, was blank. I was adrift, untethered, with nothing to anchor me. It was a strange, almost surreal feeling—like stepping off a ledge into the unknown.

So . . . what do you do when sadness takes you hostage, wrapping you in the heavy arms of loneliness?

I did what I've always done to tend to a broken heart—I sang.

But what kind of song would it be? Certainly not an achy, breaky lament. No, it had to be something that could brighten my spirit, something to gently steer my heart's compass toward happiness, even when I couldn't quite see the way. Because, after all, the tone I set now would shape the path ahead.

That night, beneath the quiet weight of it all, I shared my voice with the world for the very first time via my debut YouTube video: "Everything's Coming Up Roses."

Fitting, isn't it? I've always loved roses—their radiant elegance, their quiet resilience, how they bloom with grace, even while their thorns remain. Roses don't just flourish; they breathe life into the spaces around them, their scent capturing my heart in a way words never could.

EPILOGUE

When I reflect on my life, I see—more clearly than ever before—God's hand quietly guiding every corner and chapter. Even in the very beginning, being born in the inner city of St. Louis in the 1950s, surrounded by the vibrant culture, the rich tapestry of color, and the naturally woven diversity, I recognize His presence. As I examine the journey, including the missteps my parents made, I understand that even these moments were part of a large, divine narrative shaping who I am.

> Just as each part of the body has a different function, so we, as members of Christ, form one body with different gifts. Each of us has a unique role based on the grace given to us. If your gift is prophesying, do it in proportion to your faith; if serving, then serve; if teaching, then teach; if encouraging, then encourage; if giving, do so generously; if leading, do it diligently; and if showing mercy, do it cheerfully.
>
> —*Romans 12:4–8*

It was an indescribable blessing to be born into such a diverse and vibrant culture. I witnessed firsthand the richness of talent, the unique gifts of people, and the collaborative spirit that fueled the social and economic framework around us. There was a powerful synergy—people working together not only to help each other but also to grow their individual prosperity, meet the financial needs of their families, and collectively build something greater. We were surrounded by the blossoming of extraordinary music, a reverence for the classics, art, recreation, and the creation of hospitals, all imperfect yet striving toward something meaningful. Yes, there was greed, as there always is in human endeavors, but there was also the joy of shared culinary delights—the food and music!—and the beautiful tapestries passed down from generations. In many ways, I believe heaven will be just like that.

Luke 6:20–21 says, "Blessed are you who are poor, for yours is the kingdom of God and that they shall be satisfied and find joy."

When I reflect on my parents' lives, I see many lessons and the unmistakable hand of God moving in both of their lives. They clearly did not know how to live and made many mistakes.

First and foremost, to live a truly healthy life, we must know God. Without that foundation, how can we make sound decisions or understand the proper way to live? The scriptures remind us that God is love—unconditional, sacrificial, self-giving, merciful, compassionate, sympathetic, kind, generous, and patient. His love reaches out to us even when we fall short, for He loved us while we were still sinners. It is from His infinite goodness and mercy that He gave us a path to reconcile our sin through the redemption offered by His Son, Jesus, whom He sent to the cross for our salvation.

God is infinite—powerful, all-knowing, and eternal—the Creator of all, manifest as Father, Son, and Holy Spirit. His very essence is love, and from that love, He desires a family; this is why He created us—to love and be loved by Him. It wasn't until later in life that I truly understood that possessions, positions, accolades, or power could never bring the kind of joy that fills the deepest parts of the soul. True joy is found in relationships, especially family. But even more profound is the joy that comes from a relationship with God, our shared Father in heaven.

He is not only a God of boundless love but also of justice—both mighty and tender. He reigns with righteousness and compassion, guiding us with a perfect balance of mercy and strength. And you know what? He also has an incredible sense of humor. If you ever doubt it, take a look at His remarkable creation. The amusing antics of animals, captured in all those entertaining videos people post, are a testament to His joyful creativity. How could you not see the divine playfulness in the funny, delightful things creatures do?

My mother couldn't have possibly known my father well enough to marry him, let alone understand who God was or how to build a life based on that foundation. It takes time to truly get to know someone you plan to spend the rest of your life with and raise children alongside. However, Mom made an impulsive decision, and they both entered the marriage under false pretenses. In the beginning, they deceived one another, intentionally hiding truths that mattered. And let's not forget, omission is a form of dishonesty.

When I first purchased a business insurance policy for errors and omissions, I found myself wondering, "Why do I need coverage for something called omissions?" It clicked when I realized that omission is the act of deliberately leaving out key details to mislead or distort reality. Both my parents did just that, deceiving each other from the start, which is never a healthy foundation for a relationship.

Fast forward a bit when Mom made a monumental mistake by marrying a man she barely knew, only to discover immediately after the wedding that he was headed to jail.

What occurs when we make mistakes—particularly the significant ones? We all stumble, don't we?

Yet, God forgives us, of course! And His grace extends far beyond mere forgiveness; He utilizes these moments to mold us, to humble us, and to draw us closer to Him. Each misstep is an opportunity for redemption and a lesson in growth. God transforms our failures into lessons of reliance on His boundless grace. However, we must be willing to learn and strive to avoid repeating the same errors; life has a way of placing us back in the same classroom until we do. Through it all, He remains by our side, ready to guide us through every challenge.

But here lies the critical question: Did God love Jack?

Absolutely! His love is unconditional, welcoming anyone—everyone—to come to Him in genuine repentance. God detests sin, so Jack needed to acknowledge his wrongdoing, seek mercy, and undergo a transformation of heart and behavior. The Bible teaches us that we are all sinners, and while we were yet sinners, Christ died for us—all of us.

> For all have sinned and fall short of the glory of God.
> —*Romans 3:23*

Tragically for Jack, he never had the chance to change his path. His death came swiftly and without warning—leaving no opportunity for future repentance with a gun aimed at his head. And let's not be deceived: no confession can be made after death, and even a last-minute plea is no guarantee of salvation. For Jack, it was simply too late. What does the Bible say about salvation after death? What if someone died and, upon facing judgment, accepted Jesus as their Savior upon realizing, "Oh no! He is real"?

The Bible is quite clear: each of us must make a decision before our time on Earth concludes.

> Then I saw a great white throne and Him who was seated on it. The earth and the heavens fled from His presence, and there was no place for them. And I saw the dead, great and small, standing before the throne, and books were opened. Another book was opened, which is the book of life. The dead were judged according to what they had done as recorded in the books.
> —*Revelation 20:11–12*

> "Not everyone who says to me, 'Lord, Lord,' will enter the kingdom of heaven, but only the one who does the will of my Father who is in heaven. Many will say to me on that day, 'Lord, Lord, did we not prophesy in your name and in your name drive out demons and in your name perform many miracles?' Then I will tell them plainly, 'I never knew you. Away from me, you evildoers!'"
> —*Matthew 7:21–23*

The pressing question that weighs on my heart is: Should I forgive my mother and father, even when they intentionally caused me pain? This inquiry has troubled me throughout my life, and perhaps it resonates with you as well.

First and foremost, we are reminded of the fifth commandment in the Bible.

> Honor your father and your mother, so that you may live long in the land the Lord your God is giving you.
> —*Exodus 20:12*

This commandment stands as the first with a promise: by respecting and accepting our parents' authority and by appreciating them, we are assured that our days will be prolonged and our lives will be enriched. What could be more precious than that?

Furthermore, we are called to love one another as our Heavenly Father loves us. Forgiveness is not merely a duty; it is a profound act of love that empowers us to rise above bitterness. It nurtures our hearts and souls, reminding us of the importance of compassion. The Bible urges us to embrace forgiveness, for it is essential for our spiritual and emotional well-being.

> Then Peter came to Jesus and asked, "Lord, how many times shall I forgive my brother or sister who sins against me? Up to seven times?"
> Jesus answered, "I tell you, not seven times, but seventy-seven times."
> —*Matthew 18:21–22*

As I progress in my journey, I recognize the profound transformation that occurs when we separate ourselves from evil. This choice opens the door to a life filled with joy, happiness, and genuine fellowship. We find the freedom to be ourselves without the burden of tension. Once again, it is evident that family and friends are at the heart of true happiness. By removing negativity and malevolence from our lives, we elevate our spirits and shield ourselves from temptation, allowing our true selves to flourish in an environment of positivity and love.

The reality that my father was implicated in the murder of a realtor—and likely orchestrated it—was not beyond God's sight. I find it difficult to comprehend how some can rationalize sin; the mere thought of planning a murder should invoke the severest consequences as an expression of divine judgment.

Before my father was violently taken from this world at a young age, I believe he was granted countless opportunities to change his course, yet he repeatedly chose not to. His aggression toward my mother inflicted irreparable harm, robbing his children of a life free from pain. It is my conviction that at that moment, God's wrath descended upon him, and justice was ultimately served in his death. In a sense, God spared us from Jack's ongoing miserable existence.

Lou Wallach, the man who was acquitted, later crossed paths with my sister—the very daughter of the man he murdered. I cannot dismiss this encounter as mere coincidence. Could it be that God was reminding Lou of the need to reconcile with Him?

The life my mother had with Wayne Budde is abundant with divine lessons.

My mother often took pride in sharing tales of accumulating assets and exquisite possessions with my aunts, seizing every opportunity to showcase her successes. In doing so, she inadvertently sparked feelings of jealousy and covetousness, not only for her material wealth but also her husband.

When pride comes, then comes destruction, but with humility comes wisdom.

—*Proverbs 11:2*

The Lord detests all the proud of heart. Be sure of this: They will not go unpunished.

—*Proverbs 16:5*

My parents, though far from perfect, imparted many invaluable lessons.

Their work ethic was nothing short of extraordinary, and the dividends it paid were substantial. Hard work fosters self-esteem and sets a shining example for everyone watching, allowing us to reap benefits mentally, physically, and spiritually—even as we face the challenges of disability or retirement. You've likely heard the saying, "Use it or lose it," and it is true. A part of us fades when we stop engaging with life. Just imagine if God had decided to retire halfway through creation—perhaps before the sixth day! After all, we are wonderfully and mysteriously made in His image, which is precisely why we are valuable and must remain active at all times. Because let's face it: the universe might still be waiting for the final touches on that grand creation if He'd called it quits!

My parents' success, I believe, was largely attributed to their unwavering commitment to tithing; they never missed a single opportunity to give. God truly loves a cheerful giver, and He rewards those who faithfully offer their tithes. Personally, I've experienced the remarkable phenomenon of blessings appearing seemingly out of nowhere. When we give willingly, not out of obligation but with joy in our hearts, sharing a portion of what we earn, God promises to return those blessings in abundance. It's a divine principle that transforms generosity into overflow!

> Honor the Lord with your wealth, with the firstfruits of all your crops.
>
> —*Proverbs 3:9*

"Will a mere mortal rob God? Yet you rob me. But you ask, 'How are we robbing you?' In tithes and offerings. You are under a curse—your whole nation—because you are robbing me. Bring the whole tithe into the storehouse, that there may be food in my house. Test me in this," says the Lord Almighty, "and see if I will not throw open the floodgates of heaven and pour out so much blessing that there will not be room enough to store it. I will prevent pests from devouring your crops, and the vines in your fields will not drop their fruit before it is ripe," says the Lord Almighty.

—*Malachi 3:8–11*

Can you believe God actually says, "Test me in this"? It's the only place in Scripture where He issues such a bold invitation! It's like God's version of a dare—"Go ahead, challenge me!" If you haven't tried it yet, why not give it a shot? You might just discover that His promises are more reliable than the dividends on your stocks, which can sometimes feel as unpredictable as a rollercoaster ride!

As a young child, my parents took my sisters and me to see a traveling evangelist, a memory that has remained etched in my mind. His sermon was simple, reminiscent of the teachings of Jesus, revealing that the love of God is inherently uncomplicated.

Truth is a fundamental aspect of our human nature; there are no gray areas when it comes to right and wrong. Even young children instinctively recognize good from evil; if told to harm another child, they immediately sense the moral implications of such an action. Many pets also possess an innate awareness of right and wrong. So, why not share the straightforward truth of who Jesus is? He stands as the only perfect human to have walked this earth.

What could possibly be wrong with imparting the extraordinary message of His boundless love? Children crave depth and their souls yearn for goodness, making them eager recipients of such beautiful truths.

Train up a child in the way he should go; even when he is old he will not depart from it.

—*Proverbs 22:6*

Perhaps one of the most painful experiences of my life was being told I couldn't go to college. As I watched friends prepare for their university journeys, I felt my own unfulfilled potential press down on me. Despite knowing I was an excellent candidate, the sting of exclusion cut deep, leaving me with a profound sense of sorrow. There were moments when the ache of it all made me question the point of living. For what felt an eternity, hope seemed elusive, as if it slipped through my fingers, leaving nothing but disappointment.

First, let me emphasize the importance of understanding our children as individuals with their own feelings and needs. The Bible clearly warns against provoking them.

> Fathers, do not provoke your children; instead, bring them up in the training and instruction of the Lord.
> —*Ephesians 6:4*

This directive extends to mothers as well. To provoke means to stir up irritation or exasperation, leading children toward anger or bitterness. This manifests in various harmful ways, such as being unfair or arbitrary in meeting their needs, neglecting to offer praise, living hypocritically, imposing unrealistic expectations, or being unjustly impatient.

In my experience, pursuing an education was essential for navigating life. Yet, despite my parents' means, they kicked me out without adequately preparing me for the world. If they truly cared, they would have recognized the immense suffering their actions caused.

Indeed, while it may seem incidental, it is anything but trivial: I recognize that even though my daughter no longer lives under my roof, our bond as mother and daughter is eternal. The principles laid out in Scripture remain relevant and binding throughout life, enduring until our last breath.

What, then, should one do when faced with the burden of an unfortunate hand—a losing hand—when life doesn't provide the essentials we so desperately need?

The Scriptures never promise life will be easy. In times of pain and adversity, reach out to God, for He hears our prayers. Regular immersion in Scripture provides invaluable guidance; a Bible tucked away in your nightstand is as vital as a raincoat, umbrella, car insurance, or a reliable pair of boots. When storms arise, the pages give safety and direction. God attentively hears the prayers of the righteous.

There have been periods in life when I had to take things one day at a time, seeking divine guidance anew each day. Journaling became my companion during these times, allowing me to reflect on my progress, and I wholeheartedly encourage this practice whenever possible. But above all, persist. Never lose hope; keep moving forward. Remember, God will not give you more than you can bear. Navigating through rough patches enables us to grow and prepares us for greater responsibilities ahead. Embrace each challenge and take it as far as you can—never give up.

I realize now that I should have remained married to my first husband. Was he perfect? Certainly not, and I was far from it as well. However, divorce is seldom a wise choice; it often wreaks havoc on lives. My first husband never remarried and remained childless, a poignant reminder of the lasting impact of our separation. In the years that followed our divorce, I found myself floundering aimlessly, grappling with uncertainty. He was a steadfast partner—honest, hardworking, and dedicated. Losing that bond left a mark, a reminder of the complexities of relationships and lessons learned too late.

Throughout my journey, God graciously provided me with invaluable mentors—Betty Kraus, Michael Adachi, Judy Weltz, Dr. Safon, Mary Rydeout, and countless other seniors. They imparted wisdom on analyzing people, thriving in retirement, and navigating the intricate pathways of life. They taught me that destiny is not a mere matter of chance; it is forged through conscious choices and proactive efforts.

My time in Hollywood, surrounded by stars, revealed an essential truth: not all that glitters is gold. The glimmering facade often hides deeper struggles, and I witnessed firsthand the complexities that accompanied the lives of those I encountered.

Reflecting on Mom and Wayne's relationship, it's clear that their divorce was a profound mistake. They once epitomized the ideal marriage, yet my father's infidelity shattered that bond. Could he have sought forgiveness? Could my mother have turned to my Aunt Mary, asserting her rightful place and refusing to accept betrayal? We must champion our marriages; after all, human frailty is an inherent part of our nature.

Ultimately, my stepfather remarried a woman who succumbed to alcoholism, and he left this world too soon, disenfranchised by life and, I believe, a broken heart. My mother, on the other hand, struggled and wandered the remainder of her life, never reclaiming the joy and stability she once knew.

Along with devastating their relationship, the divorce fractured family ties; I have not spoken to my half-sister since. The aftermath of their choices resonates deeply, a reminder of the critical importance of commitment and the impact our decisions have on those we love.

Be careful what you pray for—you've likely heard that before. God may answer your prayers in ways you never imagined. For years, I fervently prayed for a child, but given the chaos and heartbreak of my relationships with men, I never envisioned a husband in that picture. I longed for a quiet life with just my child and me. In the end, that's exactly what I got. But perhaps, had I truly studied the Scriptures and understood the character of a godly husband, I would have seen that what I needed wasn't one of the men I had known, but a fine, godly man. Maybe then, my prayer—and my life—would have been far healthier.

However, I learned a hard lesson about intimacy without commitment, especially when alcohol enters the mix. Engaging in such vulnerability can lead us down perilous paths. While one dance may seem innocent enough, multiple dances can invite a sexual allure that puts us at risk. Alcohol doesn't just cloud our judgment; it also accelerates the aging process.

When we stray from God's path and indulge in sin, it can feel exhilarating in the moment. But when it's time to face the consequences, there's rarely a grand spectacle. Instead, we find ourselves caught in the quiet aftermath of our choices, a stark reminder of the gravity of our actions.

One of the most pivotal experiences in my life that led me to a deeper relationship with Jesus was my journey to Boston to see Mr. Carter. As I embarked on that long train ride north, I found myself engrossed in a book titled *Babylon Mystery*. At the time, I couldn't fathom why God would direct me to Boston, especially after fervently praying for a job that never materialized. I was angry with God, feeling He had let me down.

However, looking back, I see the divine hand at work. On that train, buried in frustration, I delved into the pages of that book. The veil was torn away by that book, revealing profound truths that changed my life forever. What the enemy intended for harm, God transformed into something beautiful. I would never have taken the time to study one of my mother's Christian books willingly, but, lo and behold, it was all I had at my disposal. Imagine that! It's funny how God works, turning unwanted reading material into our greatest revelations. Who knew a train ride could lead to divine enlightenment? Next time I'll pack a suitcase full of books and take the express route to enlightenment!

When I first interviewed with Lasell College and received a disappointing "No," I was disheartened. But that experience taught me an invaluable lesson about prayer and patience. When you ask for something, remember that God's timing is often different from our own. He may be testing your resolve. Sometimes, the answer comes later, just as it did for me when they called me back, ultimately offering me my dream job. So, when faced with setbacks, hold on to your faith; you never know when the door will swing wide open!

As I reflect on that fateful day when I was so close to being sent to the World Trade Center to complete my training on 9/11, I can't help but marvel at God's intervention. I was ready to bring my daughter along, but my boss advised me to wait. Who knows what might have happened? I am eternally grateful for that divine delay.

My story would not be complete without acknowledging the awe-inspiring providence of God, along with His righteous wrath against those who do wrong. Take, for instance, the infamous Joe Romano—a pariah who promised to help my daughter with her college expenses only to later deny her that assistance. Little did he know that his deceitful actions would come to light through my own discovery on the computer. It's truly fascinating how fate intervened: not only was our divorce settlement substantial enough to cover Rachel's tuition at her dream school, UCSB, and her sorority expenses, but it also provided me with enough resources to reclaim my life.

Isn't it remarkable? God works in mysterious ways to demonstrate His infinite love and ensure we are never forsaken. His hand guides us through trials and tribulations, turning moments of despair into triumphs, reminding us that even the most difficult situations can lead to greater blessings. And that, dear reader, is the incredible journey of faith that continues to unfold in my life.